International politics in Europe

Throughout much of Europe the preoccupation with military security that dominated political thinking after the end of the Second World War has given way to an emphasis upon mutual interdependence. But what does this mean, both theoretically and practically, in terms of a 'new' agenda?

The focus of this book is upon four main issues: economic development; security; the environment; and human rights. These are of course not in themselves new issues, but during the period of the Cold War they were subordinated to the ideological division of the continent. Now they have emerged as decisive in the way in which Europe will develop.

The authors examine the four issues in depth, and draw out the links between them. They also examine the various levels at which these problems exist - the level of the system, of the state and of the individual. Thus it is possible for them to illustrate general issues with specific reference to local, national and Europe-wide political debates.

G. Wyn Rees is a lecturer in International Relations at the University of Leicester.

Green Political Thought
Andrew Dobson

Searching for the New France
James F. Hollifield and *George Ross* (eds)

Integration and Co-operation in Europe
Brigid Laffan

Perspectives on World Politics
Richard Little and *Mike Smith* (eds)

Security and Strategy in the New Europe
Colin McInnes (ed.)

The Evolution of International Society
Adam Watson

After 1992
Ernest Wistrich

The Government and Politics of France (3rd edn)
Vincent Wright

International politics in Europe

The new agenda

Edited by G. Wyn Rees

ROUTLEDGE

London and New York

First published 1993
by Routledge
11 New Fetter Lane, London EC4P 4EE

Simultaneously published in the USA and Canada
by Routledge
29 West 35th Street, New York, NY 10001

© 1993 G. Wyn Rees

Typeset in Bembo by Michael Mepham, Frome, Somerset
Printed and bound in Great Britain by
Mackays of Chatham PLC, Chatham, Kent.

British Library Cataloguing in Publication Data
A catalogue record for this book is available from the British Library.
　ISBN 0–415–08282–X (hbk)
　　　 0–415–08283–8 (pbk) ·

Library of Congress Cataloging in Publication Data
International politics in Europe : the new agenda / edited by G. Wyn
Rees.
　p.　cm.
Includes bibliographical references and index.
ISBN 0–415–08282–X (hbk) : $55.00 (US).
ISBN 0–415–08283–8 (pbk) : $16.95 (US).
1. Europe—Politics and government—1989–
I. Rees. G. Wyn, 1963– .
D2009.I64　1993
940.55'9—dc20　　　　　　　　　　　　　　 92–44820
　　　　　　　　　　　　　　　　　　　　　 CIP

*This book is dedicated to my
mother and father, Marian and Bryan*

Contents

Figures and tables

FIGURES

TABLES

Contributors

David Armstrong is Senior Lecturer in International Organisation at the University of Birmingham.

R. J. Barry Jones is a Lecturer in International Relations at the University of Reading.

Stuart Croft is Senior Lecturer in Security Studies at the University of Birmingham.

Adrian Hyde-Price is a Lecturer in the Department of Politics at the University of Southampton.

Colin McInnes is a Lecturer in the Department of International Politics at the University College of Wales, Aberystwyth.

G. Wyn Rees is a Lecturer in International Relations at the University of Leicester.

David Sadler is a Lecturer in European Politics at De Montfort University, Leicester.

Joanna Spear is the Director of the Graduate School of International Studies at the University of Sheffield.

Nicholas Wheeler is a Lecturer in the Department of Politics at the University of Hull.

Part I

Levels of analysis

Chapter 1

Introduction

G. Wyn Rees

Einstein once said that everything was changed by the explosion of the atomic bomb except humankind's way of thinking about things. A similar thing could be said to have occurred in European politics following the end of the Cold War. With the collapse of the Warsaw Pact and the subsequent disintegration of the Soviet Union, the traditional bloc structure in Europe was brought to an end. Yet to change the way we approach and seek to understand politics in the region will not happen quickly. A mind-set that was four decades in the making will have to be altered. The rapidity and complexity of developments since that time have added to the difficulties. Time has not been available for reflection and for the full implications of the changes in European politics to be digested. The task of developing new ways of thinking about post-Cold War politics in Europe is still in its infancy.

The Europe of the Cold War was relatively simple to understand. It had remained largely static for a long time. Its origins lay in the Yalta Conference of February 1945 when the 'Big Three' allied powers began to turn their attention from the strategy of the war to the shape of the peace. With the failure to resolve the disagreements between them and a growing suspicion of the intentions of the Soviet Union by the United States and Great Britain, the continent gradually became the focus of a bitter ideological division. Two antithetical political and social systems emerged, neatly labelled 'east' and 'west', and were codified in the Helsinki Final Act of 1975. This gave legitimacy to the *de facto* territorial changes that had taken place during the 1939–45 war.

Cold War Europe was overshadowed by two superpowers whose interests dictated the political agenda. America's policy of containing the Soviet Union by military means and the desire of post-war Soviet leaders to provide for the absolute security of their country, ensured that the continent was divided into hostile blocs. These blocs became an important part of the status of the superpowers and as a result they expended a considerable amount of effort in obtaining conformity within their spheres. In the east this was achieved through tight political control and occasionally brute force; whilst in the west, the United States was able to exercise leadership as a result of her predominant economic and military strength.

Military security issues dominated the political agenda during this time as Europe was the 'front-line' of the east–west confrontation. The North Atlantic Treaty Organisation (NATO) and the Warsaw Treaty Organisation (WTO) confronted each other across the inner-German border and the possibility of a Soviet armoured attack across the North German Plain preoccupied the minds of western leaders. In the midst of this highly threatening situation, nuclear weapons ensured that a stalemate existed. The possession of these weapons by both sides made it likely that a conflict would quickly escalate to a catastrophic level of destruction in which neither side could achieve victory. The vast majority of the nuclear weapons were held by the two superpowers and this perpetuated their hegemonic position on the continent. Such a situation had the advantage of being stable but it took no account of the wishes of the peoples of eastern Europe.

As a consequence of the particular importance attached to military security during the Cold War, other issues were relegated to a subordinate position. Matters that concerned European countries, such as the process of economic integration flowing from the Treaty of Rome in 1957, and the degree of communication between the two halves of Europe, were made subordinate to the security agenda. Furthermore, not only were such subjects relegated in importance, but they were often treated as security issues, thereby lying within the purview of the superpowers. For example, west European integration was regarded by the United States at different times as either a vital prerequisite to the cohesion of the west or as a potential threat to the leadership role of the US.

This then was the Cold War system that dominated Europe, but there was evidence by the 1970s that this system might not last forever. A period of *détente* developed between the superpowers and was given substance by arms control agreements and summit meetings (Williams and Bowker 1988). This provided a framework in which trade and cultural contacts between the two halves of Europe were able to proliferate and hence a European form of *détente* was born. Germany was at the forefront of this change in Europe, through Chancellor Brandt's policy of 'Ostpolitik', that had awaited an improvement in east–west relations. The European form of *détente* delivered real benefits, such as trade, more freedom of movement and cultural contacts. This proved to be of greater value to the European states than the *rapprochement* between the superpowers. When the US and USSR began to return to a confrontational stance in the early 1980s, there was a reluctance in Europe to follow suit. The states of west and eastern Europe were less willing to have their interests dictated to them by their respective superpower guardians.

This process had reached a relatively more advanced stage in western Europe. *Détente* had encouraged more self-reliance amongst the European members of NATO and prompted a host of arguments with the United States. These included resentment from within the US over the distribution of burdens within the Alliance and the perception that the Europeans were not carrying their fair share. The west Europeans were mistrustful of the American commitment to extended nuclear deterrence and tension arose around the deployment of new land-based Cruise and Pershing II missiles. The apparent insensitivity of the Reagan administration towards their interests unsettled European governments. This was particularly acute over the insistence by Washington that trade relations with the east should be sacrificed due to the security implications: the Trans-Siberian gas pipeline is a good example. Even a state such as West Germany, dependent on American security guarantees and traditionally loyal to Washington, was loath to sacrifice the gains it had made with eastern Europe in the preceding decade.

As US policy towards the Soviet Union during the second Reagan term changed to constructive engagement, this did not resolve the intra-allied tensions. Criticism then arose of the inconsistency of American policy amid fear that deals would be done by the superpowers over the heads of the Europeans. Justification for this fear was to be found at the Reykjavik meeting between Reagan and Gorbachev in 1986. Without the prior agreement of his western allies, the American President discussed the possibility of eliminating all ballistic missiles within ten years (Sharp 1987). Clearly, this would have had enormous implications for the security policies of west European states. Such events seemed to be symptomatic of the growing estrangement between the US and its closest allies.

Although not as overt as the changes in the west, important developments had occurred in the relationship between east European countries and the Soviet Union by the latter 1980s. The regimes in the east had always lacked domestic legitimacy, partly as a consequence of their failure to satisfy the consumer demands of their population. Therefore they still relied heavily upon support from Moscow to retain their positions. They acquiesced, somewhat grudgingly, in the scaling down of contacts with western Europe during the years of the New Cold War because it was demanded by Moscow. Like their western counterparts, they had valued the better relationship between the two halves of the continent. This was not because it had improved human rights, but because it had led to soft loans and the importation of foreign goods. Countries such as Poland had been able to amass considerable debts to western banks during the period of *détente* and were reluctant to sacrifice these contacts to appease the Soviet Union. Figures such as Erich Honecker in the German Democratic Republic (GDR) had made it clear that they viewed the deterioration in east–west relations as only a temporary set-back.

However, a far more decisive development had taken place in Moscow since 1985. The accession to power of Mikhail Gorbachev heralded a reappraisal of the value of an unreformed eastern bloc to Soviet interests. This process led to the recognition that the satellite states had grown into a serious drain on the Soviet economy which, in view of its weakness, could no longer be tolerated. Allied to this were two other considerations. One was a strategic reassessment that rejected the aged assumption that the bloc was a vital security barrier to the USSR and that its military importance was always paramount. The second was a desire by Moscow to decrease tension with the west to facilitate domestic reconstruction. This was pursued through a policy of negotiation with the United States and by emphasising the Soviet Union's claim to be part of a 'Common European Home' (Gorbachev 1988). The courting of western Europe reflected a desire to secure economic aid and technical assistance in the modernisation of the east.

Gorbachev recognised that the 'restructuring' of the Soviet economy would demand a fundamentally different relationship with the states of eastern Europe. As reform in the Soviet Union gathered momentum, the leadership came to realise that economic modernisation could not be achieved without greater political freedom or 'openness' (glasnost). Yet the implications of these changes for eastern Europe do not appear to have been fully thought through: the regimes were fragile, corrupt and dependent upon Moscow for their legitimacy. Some states had already undergone change. Hungary, for example, had made considerable efforts to change itself, whilst Poland's reform process had been pushed along by the Solidarity movement. Other regimes, however, such as Honecker's in the GDR, attempted to set their faces against the reform process in the Soviet Union, but without the support of their superpower patron, their positions were largely untenable.

Hence, even before the events of 1989, there was evidence that the relationship between the USSR and its eastern satellites was in a process of transition. There was also evidence of structural changes between east and western Europe that are worthy of mention. The east had become a good deal more open to western ideas due to the larger amount of travel across the continent and as a result of the penetration of western television and media. The east had become more economically interdependent and less isolated and a transmission belt had developed for western technology through the northern tier states of the eastern bloc to the Soviet Union itself. This increased interaction between the blocs was best symbolised by the GDR which enjoyed a unique role as an associate member of the European Community, thanks to its relationship with the Federal Republic of Germany (FRG).

When the revolutions of 1989 did come, they swept away the governments of the east with breathtaking speed. It will probably never be known to what extent the Soviet Union supported the changes in governments in eastern Europe or whether it just misjudged the situation. It is likely that after acting as a catalyst for the reform process, Moscow was unable to keep up with the rapidity of events and the crisis spiralled out of its control. The Soviet leadership could never have foretold that the early protest marches in the city of Leipzig would culminate in the unification of Germany and the collapse of the Warsaw Treaty Organisation. Where the Soviet government did play a crucial role was in declaring before the revolutions that it would not use force in eastern Europe to oppose political change, as it had done so ruthlessly in Hungary in 1956 and in Czechoslovakia in 1968. Undeniably, this was a reassuring factor for the opposition movements in eastern Europe because it removed the threat that Soviet tanks might crush their protests. Gorbachev proved true to his word as Soviet troops stood passively aside as the unpopular regimes toppled in rapid succession.

The removal of the governments of the east European states and the democratisation of their political structures has changed the face of the region. The revolutions overtook the incremental process of fragmentation and served to undermine the entire bloc structure at a stroke. It became only a matter of time before the military and economic frameworks that legitimised Soviet control in the east, the Warsaw Pact and the Council for Mutual Economic Assistance (CMEA), were rendered defunct. Without their close bilateral ties to the Soviet Union, east European governments found themselves in a security and trading vacuum. This problem has been compounded by the lack of government experience of many of these new leaders. They now looked to western states rather than to the east, to provide them with assistance and solutions to their difficulties.

Presidents Bush and Gorbachev at their summit off Malta in December 1989 declared that the ideological division of Europe was over. The implications for western Europe of the changes in the east were enormous.

The perception of threat that had provided the glue for states within both the western alliance and the European Community was removed. In the past American leadership of the west could be justified on grounds of military security, but this was no longer necessary. The way was open, after consultations between the former occupying powers, for the unification of Germany to take place and for agreement over the removal of Soviet forces from the GDR by 1994. The politico-economic landscape at the heart of the continent was transformed and the superpowers were no longer the dominant voices in European affairs.

With the collapse of the Soviet Union, the demotion of military security issues on the continent was complete. This is not to suggest that this issue is no longer important – conflict is still a reality in post-Cold War Europe – but it is no longer in a dominant position. Now, greater attention can be payed to the plethora of other issues that were relegated to positions of secondary importance during the Cold War.

A NEW EUROPEAN AGENDA

This book seeks to put forward the argument that a different series of issues can now be discerned on the European agenda. The Cold War period was so dominated by the issue of military security that other important issues were relatively neglected. Now that fear of a major conflict has receded, a variety of other issues have emerged into the limelight. These issues are not new, some in fact pre-date the Cold War, but they have hitherto been accorded a subordinate position. The end of the Cold War has both influenced the nature of these issues and enabled them to receive the attention that they deserve. The new issue agenda is broader and more complex than that which it replaces.

Four issues now dominate this agenda. First is the issue of security following the collapse of the adversarial bloc structures between east and west. Security must now be defined in a different way to take account of the changed risks on the continent. The second concerns the manner and speed of economic development in Europe. This subsumes the pressing question of the reconstruction of the economies in eastern Europe and the process of greater economic integration in both east and west. The third issue is the need to tackle environmental degradation and the evolving tension between economic growth and the environment. Fourthly and finally is the issue of human rights in the new Europe and the dilemmas over developing criteria for humanitarian intervention.

It is also the contention of this book that these issues have a distinctive regional identity. That is to say that they are pan-European in nature, transcending the old east–west divide in Europe. Just as analysts must take account of a revised issue agenda, so they must study these subjects across the continent as a whole. These issues reflect the interdependence of Europe. For example, it now makes little sense to look at the military security problem through the old conceptual lens of the Cold War, when states in the east are seeking to join western security institutions such as NATO. Issues like these need to be addressed across the whole of Europe, demanding a change in the way Europe is studied. Clearly there remain major differences between the states of the former halves of Europe, but the issues they face are common to both and solutions to problems will have to take account of this.

In adopting this focus the book will lay itself open to the criticism that it neglects the residual influence in Europe of the United States and the heirs of the former Soviet Union. Both the US and Russia have signalled their intention to continue to play a role in Europe and the influence of these states in European affairs is still considerable. In December 1989, Secretary of State James Baker professed an American desire to perpetuate long-established ties with western Europe when he called for the establishment of a 'New Atlanticism' (US Information Service 1989). However, this book argues that the new agenda of issues will not lend itself easily to direction and interference from states outside the region. In the past, the defence issue demanded that outside powers – the Soviet Union and the United States – played a major role. In the future, issues such as economic integration and pollution control will not be legitimate matters for external interference.

States within the region will therefore have to find their own solutions to the problems raised by these issues. The obvious disparities of size and strength between states within the region will be reflected in the differing abilities to deal with these problems. The opportunity to look outside the region for assistance, even if states should wish to do so, will be limited. The United States is likely to be preoccupied with its own problems such as reducing its vast budget deficit and improving its balance of trade with Japan. Russia, with its economy in ruins and its political stability uncertain, will be seeking assistance from countries such as Germany, rather than providing help from its own resources.

The post-Cold War continent is still in a process of transition and attempting to define the boundaries of this new Europe is fraught with difficulty. Following the revolutions of 1989, it was convenient to regard the boundary of Europe as lying on the eastern edge of Poland, in order to differentiate it from the territory of the Soviet Union. Yet with the disintegration of the latter state and the proliferation of new republics that wish to be included within the European family, and more particularly within western institutions, the definition of Europe has become more problematic. The focus of this book is upon Europe from Portugal to Poland, whilst recognising that states outside this area also have a bearing upon the issues that are discussed. A more detailed attempt to come to terms with this problem is made in Chapter 2.

AIMS AND STRUCTURE

The book is divided into two parts to ensure its accessibility at both undergraduate and postgraduate level. Before looking at the four issues of military security, economics, the environment and human rights, the reader is introduced in the first part to three levels of analysis. It is no longer sufficient to study the politics of the continent at the level of the state only, as if this actor remained all-competent. Instead, it is necessary to appreciate that both problems and solutions in the new Europe will exist on several levels - above and below the level of states. Hence Part I will investigate the system, state and individual levels of analyses, contrasting how the Europe of today differs with that of the Cold War period. Furthermore, it will be possible to see how the new agenda of issues are developing on these various levels and how solutions to problems will need to take account of these levels.

The system level chapter by Adrian Hyde-Price looks at the European state system during the Cold War and compares it to the emerging Europe of today, with its blurred edges and regional groupings. Hyde-Price proceeds to analyse the supranational organisations which are likely to play a central role in managing the issues outlined in the second section of the book. He introduces a number of debates that appear throughout the book; namely the trend towards east European problems requiring western solutions and the attempt to draw former states of the eastern bloc into institutionalised cooperation.

The state level chapter by David Sadler contrasts the reassertion of nation-state structures in the eastern half of the continent after 1989, with the moves to integration in the western half through the vehicle of the European Community (EC). He analyses the relative distribution of power in Europe and cautions against an overly simplistic approach to the trends of state-building and integration in the two halves of the continent. After all, in the east, there are powerful forces of economic strife and ethnic conflict which are ripping states apart; whilst in the west, Sadler questions whether the advancement of the EC necessarily implies a diminution of the authority of the nation-state.

The individual level chapter by David Armstrong and Stuart Croft looks at the debate during the Cold War between individual rights in western Europe versus collective rights in the east. The authors then assess the implications of the apparent triumph of the western view after the end of the Cold War, that political and civil rights take priority over social and economic rights. The chapter raises the interesting question of to what extent western models may be considered appropriate to remedy eastern problems.

Part II of this book switches attention to the new agenda of issues in Europe. Although no attempt is made to rank the issues in order of importance, there is a progression from the better known to the less well-discussed issues. Reference is made in each of the issue chapters to the multiple levels on which these problems exist.

Colin McInnes presents the first chapter on the military security issue within Part II. He questions the way security ought to be understood after the Cold War, broadening the concept to include human rights, economic well-being and the environment. Attention is drawn to the greater volatility of some regions in Europe now that bloc hegemony has disappeared. He warns against an expectation that military intervention by one state in the internal affairs of another will necessarily increase, due to the potentially high cost and risk of failure.

The next chapter, by R. J. Barry Jones, investigates the economic development of the continent and focuses, specifically, on the European Community. The future expansion of the EC is addressed in detail along with the ramifications of such a development on the process of integration and EC relations with the rest of the world. The problems of eastern Europe receive attention, as well as the existing imbalance of economic strength within the Community.

Joanna Spear's chapter on environmental issues contrasts the debate that is taking place in west and eastern Europe over damage to the environment and the optimum responses. Spear looks at the diplomacy that has taken place over this subject and the relationship between economic development and the environment.

The final chapter in Part II, by Nicholas Wheeler, looks at the issue of human rights and the legitimacy of humanitarian intervention. He focuses upon the case study of the crisis in former Yugoslavia and assesses whether humanitarian intervention can be reconciled with the security needs of the new Europe. He analyses the roles played by the Conference on Security and Cooperation in Europe (CSCE) and the EC in that crisis.

In the conclusion, an attempt is made to illustrate some of the ways in which the issues interlink with one another and how the problems manifest themselves in different forms in the two halves of the continent. There is no agreed view over how the continent will develop in even the medium term, let alone the long-term future.

Chapter 2

The system level
The changing topology of Europe
Adrian G. V. Hyde-Price

INTRODUCTION

Since the final years of the 1980s, once unimaginable events have transformed the face of Europe. After four decades of Cold War stability, the 'old continent' has experienced change on a scale only previously associated with major wars or revolutionary upheavals, such as 1789, 1917–8 or 1939. This cascade of changes has profoundly and irrevocably transformed the topology of power relations from Vancouver to Vladivostock. Alliances and multilateral organisations have collapsed whilst others have been transformed or invigorated; Germany – traditionally the key to the European balance of power – has reunited, without war or a significant international crisis; a nuclear superpower has fragmented, without widespread bloodshed; new states have been born as others have disintegrated; and new patterns of cooperation and conflict have emerged in a Europe no longer divided into two hostile and antagonistic blocs. Moreover, as Europe's politics have changed, its geographical boundaries have become even more blurred: today, more than ever before in the past, it has become extremely difficult to specify where 'Europe' ends, and 'Asia' begins. Above all, however, it is the structural dynamics of Europe at the systemic level which have changed. In any distinct geographical area (however imprecise its boundaries), relations between states and peoples form a unique tapestry of complex interactions. This tapestry is more than just the sum of its parts: it generates a dynamic of its own, which in turn affects the behaviour of its constituent elements.[1] K. J. Holsti has defined an international system as 'any collection of independent political entities . . . that interact with considerable frequency and according to regularised processes' (Holsti 1983: 27). The existence of a specific international system in Europe is particularly apparent, given the intensity of the transnational and international interdependencies in the continent. To give one example: it is hardly possible to explain the rationale behind British or

German defence policy in a particular period without reference to the structure of the European interstate system of the time. The interstate system in Europe should therefore be seen as just that, a system – defined by the overall pattern of interlocking and overlapping relationships and institutions, and with its own internal logic and structural dynamics. It is above all these structural dynamics of the European state system that have changed as the pattern of power relations in the continent has sharply altered over recent years.

The concern of this chapter, therefore, is to describe the changes which have taken place in Europe at the system level, and to explore the implications of these changes for the future evolution of the continent in the post-Cold War world. Let us begin by considering the nature of the bipolar system which, by and large, held Europe in its icy grip for almost forty years.

THE EUROPEAN STATE SYSTEM IN THE COLD WAR

The bipolar system of the Cold War years was as stable as it was unacceptable. It was stable because of the cohesion it engendered in the two rival and antagonistic blocs, and because the nuclear standoff upon which it was based made the costs of any attempt to force change in the system disproportionate to any hoped-for gains. Yet it was at the same time unacceptable: unacceptable, not necessarily to the diplomats and politicians on either side, to whom stability and predictability are welcome traits of any international system. But unacceptable to the peoples of central and eastern Europe, above all to the citizens of the German Democratic Republic (GDR) – whose dignified and peaceful assertion of their democratic rights to self-determination in October 1989 sounded the final death-knell of the bipolar system.

This bipolar system of the Cold War era exhibited five defining characteristics, which distinguished it from any previous state system in the continent. The first was the dominant – not to say hegemonic – role of the two superpowers. In the immediate aftermath of the Second World War, the weakness of Europe's traditional great powers left a power vacuum which was filled by the continent's two flanking superpowers, the USA and the USSR. These two hegemons effectively determined the character of the post-war bipolar system in Europe, and their bilateral relationship was for much of the Cold War period a key determinant of the system's structural dynamics. In western Europe, the presence of what one commentator has called Europe's American 'pacifier' (Joffe 1984), helped suppress traditional nationalist rivalries in the region. This, along with the existence of a widely held perception of a common external enemy (the Soviet Union), made possible a relatively speedy post-war *rapprochement* between former combatants – most notably, France and the Federal Republic of Germany (FRG). The US influence in 'West European' (using the term in a political, rather than geographical, sense) affairs was also felt in the eastern Mediterranean, where bitter emnities between Christian Greece and Muslim Turkey – both North Atlantic Treaty Organisation (NATO) 'allies' – were to some extent at least mediated and managed by the USA.

In eastern Europe, the all-pervasive influence of the 'Land of Lenin' in the internal affairs of 'fraternal socialist allies' was particularly marked in the Stalin years. None the less, it was all too evident in 1968 when Warsaw Pact forces brutally suppressed Dubcek's attempt to forge 'socialism with a human face'. The suffocating presence of the Soviet Union in the affairs of eastern Europe suppressed ethno-national conflicts in the region (for example, between Hungary and Romania, or Poland and the GDR), but did not lead to any resolution of the underlying tensions. Thus both superpowers were able to decisively shape developments in their respective 'sphere of interest': however, this apparent symmetry does not mean that the role of the USA in western Europe was in any way comparable to that of the Soviet Union in eastern Europe. To give one striking example: whereas America's ultimate sanction when embroiled in a dispute with its European allies was to threaten to withdraw its forces, for the Soviets their ultimate sanction was to send the tanks in!

The second key feature of the bipolar system was that it rested on two rivalrous military-political alliances, each based on different socio-economic structures: in the west, under the 'benign hegemony' (Calleo 1989) of the Americans, NATO and the Economic Community (EC) were established; in the east, under the much more constricting domination of the Soviet Union, the Warsaw Pact and the Council for Mutual Economic Assistance (CMEA).

Thirdly, Germany – the lynch-pin of the European state system since the 1648 Treaty of Westphalia – was divided, each part of the divided nation being integrated into one or other of the two alliance systems under the watchful eye of their respective Superpower patron. By the 1970s, both German states had become key players in their respective alliance systems. The FRG was NATO's front-line state, and acted as host to hundreds of thousands of allied forces on the central Front. West Germany also played a key leadership role in the EC (in tandem with France), and by the 1980s the Deutschmark had developed into the anchor currency for the European Exchange Rate Mechanism. Similarly, by the 1970s the GDR had become the lynch-pin of the Soviet position in eastern Europe: both because of its military contribution to the Warsaw Pact, and because of its relatively successful economic performance within the CMEA.

Fourthly, between the two blocs was a small but distinct group of neutral and non-aligned states. Although the historical roots and political justifications for their neutrality varied immensely, they constituted a distinct grouping, which from the mid-1970s onwards played a not insignificant role as mediators between NATO and the Warsaw Pact (particularly in the framework of the Conference on Security and Cooperation in Europe).

Finally, the whole structure was underpinned by the threat of a nuclear Armaggedon. With the dawning of the nuclear age, traditional calculations concerning the rationality of using military force to achieve desired political ends became redundant. Clausewitz once described war as 'the continuation of politics by other means'. But given the awesome destructive capabilities of nuclear weapons, war between nuclear armed states or alliances could no longer be a rational instrument of policy. The danger that any armed conflict between NATO and Warsaw Pact members could lead to a full-scale nuclear exchange made political leaders in both east and west much more wary about sabre-rattling or confrontational behaviour. The existence of nuclear weapons, and the doctrines of nuclear deterrence that grew up around them, thus ironically brought an element of military stability to the east–west conflict in Europe.

These were the five key features of the system which existed in Europe for almost forty years. It congealed in the fateful years 1947–9, and, perhaps paradoxically, was stabilised by the twin crises of 1961 and 1962 (over Berlin and Cuba). During the 1970s, the political dynamics of the bipolar rivalry on which the system rested were codified by the Helsinki Final Act of 1975, which gave birth to the CSCE. The apparent stability of the system was most marked in central Europe, where the bulk of the two alliance's military hardware was concentrated. On the 'peripheries', the dynamics of the European Cold War system were modified by the persistence of strong regional factors. In the north, a unique 'Nordic balance' was identified by commentators, in which two neutral states, Finland and Sweden, existed alongside three NATO countries (Norway, Denmark and Iceland) as well as their regional 'big brother', the Soviet Union. In the south-east of Europe, another unique balance existed, with two non-aligned communist states (Yugoslavia and Albania), two Warsaw Pact countries (Bulgaria and Romania) and two NATO members (Greece and Turkey). Once again, in this region, the specific dynamics of Balkan politics distorted the impact of the east–west conflict – at times quite dramatically, as the armed conflict between the two NATO 'allies', Greece and Turkey, over Cyprus, demonstrated all too starkly.

This bipolar system appeared so stable and immutable that some commentators suggested that, however undesirable morally and politically, it actually met the functional needs of the European state system. Anton De Porte, for example, argued that the east–west system provided a functional solution to the intractable problem which destroyed the peace of Europe three times within seventy years – namely, how to integrate the rising power of a united Germany into the existing balance of power system. As he wrote in 1978:

> I think the post-war system, built over a decade and more of acute tensions sometimes threatening war, can yet be given high marks for providing stability, even if in a sense inadvertently, and at least fair marks for the kind of stability. In any case this system, like all that prove viable, has been well rooted in power realities. If not an inevitable outcome of history, it was at least a natural one. . . . I suggest that the system which has lasted from 1955 until today – 1978 – may well last as long again, that is, until 2001.
>
> (DePorte 1979: xii–xiii)

Other commentators pointed out that the Cold War brought a degree of stability to Europe because it helped suppress ancient national, ethnic and religious conflicts, and because – in western Europe at least, under the benign hegemony of Europe's 'American pacifier' (Joffe 1984) – it encouraged a process of post-war reconciliation and economic integration. Moreover, Michael Cox has actually described the Cold War itself as a 'system', arguing that the carefully controlled rivalry between the two superpowers was welcome to them as a way of bringing some predictability to the otherwise anarchic international system (Cox 1986).

Yet the stability of the bipolar system was clearly over-estimated. With the benefit of hindsight we can see that from the early 1970s onwards – despite its surface tranquility – the very foundations of the post-war European system were being ineluctably eroded by a series of powerful subterranean currents. In order to understand the nature of Europe's structural dynamics today, it is useful to briefly analyse the secular forces which led to disintegration of the Cold War system.

THE DISINTEGRATION OF THE POST-WAR BIPOLAR SYSTEM

The character of the European state system which emerged in the wake of the Second World War reflected the socio-political conditions in Europe at the time, along with the structure of the international system. In the late 1940s, much of continental Europe lay in ruins. People's expectations were low, their lives difficult and uncertain. Throughout vast areas of central and eastern Europe, as well as in many peripheral regions in western Europe, the level of economic development remained low, whilst rates of illiteracy were frustratingly high. Social inequalities and economic difficulties contributed to the substantial levels of electoral support for communist and other left-wing political parties. This in turn seemed to threaten the stability of the new regimes which emerged from the ashes of fascism and occupation. On the international level, Europe's traditional great powers were all shadows of their former selves. This left the two flanking powers with a decisive voice in the affairs of the continent (as Alexis de Tocqueville had predicted with amazing foresight in the 1830s).[2]

Given these conditions, it is understandable that the European state system developed the five distinctive characteristics enumerated above. The two alliance systems, as well as the two German states, were bound to be shaped primarily by the two superpowers given the weakness of the European states. And the establishment of communist governments in economically underdeveloped societies marked by a high degree of illiteracy and a non-participatory political culture was relatively easy, particularly when some sections of the population actively embraced the communist promise of an historical short-cut to modernity and societal progress.

The post-war state system was thus the progeny of the specific domestic and international conditions which existed in Europe in the late 1940s – early 1950s. However, the structure of power relations produced at this time was subsequently undermined by a series of secular trends which reflected changing economic, social and cultural forces.

These forces, which operated at both a domestic and an international level, can be summarised as follows: first, the growing prosperity and integration of western Europe. Thanks in no small part to the enlightened self-interest of the Americans (in the form of Marshall Aid), western Europe recovered fairly quickly in the early 1950s, and was soon enjoying rising standards of living. This growing prosperity was accompanied by a process of post-war reconciliation and deepening integration – focused above all on the European Community.

Secondly, the changing nature of the transatlantic relationship. As a consequence of western Europe's growing prosperity and cohesion, US power has – in relative terms – declined *vis-à-vis* that of its transatlantic allies. There is already a substantial body of literature on the notion of the 'decline' (relative or otherwise) of American power, and this is not the place to re-open this debate. Suffice it to say, the USA remains a major actor in global and European affairs, but its influence and standing has declined in relative terms over the last twenty years. It no longer enjoys the political influence or economic leverage it exercised in the first two decades of the post-war era (Kennedy 1988: 665).

Thirdly, the systemic failure of communism – 'the god that failed'. From 1956 onwards, it became increasingly clear that the emancipatory promises of Marxism–Leninism were as hollow and lifeless as Lenin's embalmed body. By the early 1980s, the comprehensive failure of communist regimes was blatantly evident from their political illegitimacy, economic stagnation, social decay, environmental degradation and spiritual crisis.

Fourthly, the gathering crisis in the USSR. If America's decline was relative, then that of the Soviet Union was absolute. With the benefit of hindsight, we can see that the 1979 invasion of Afghanistan marked the highwater point of Soviet expansionism. But even at this decisive moment in the exercise of its military power-projection capabilities, the Soviet system itself was terminally ill. Its political arteries were becoming sclerotic, its economic sinews had hardened to the point of paralysis, and – like a patient consumed from within by cancer – the Soviet Union was visibly dying. Gorbachev's brief when he came to office in 1985 was to preserve the USSR as a superpower in the twenty-first century, but even with all his consumate political skills, this was a miracle he could not achieve. Indeed, the effect of Gorbachev's reform programme was – by a bitter twist of fate – not to rejuvenate Soviet socialism, but to accelerate the economic decline of the Soviet Union, to unleash the centrifugal forces of nationalism and to undermine the authority of all the old institutions of the Soviet power system – the All-Union ministries in Moscow, the 'Committee of State Security' (KGB), the Communist Party of the Soviet Union (CPSU) and the Soviet Army. The August coup was a desperate tragi-comic attempt to preserve the old structures of Soviet power, but in the end it only precipitated the final demise of the USSR.

Thus by the late 1980s, the foundations of the European state system had been badly eroded. Despite its superficial look of permanence, the whole structure had become hollow and fragile. A system whose foundations were laid down in the late 1940s no longer corresponded to the domestic or international realities of the 1980s. In the end it was Gorbachev's policies of glasnost and perestroika (his forelorn attempt to revitalise the Soviet Union – one of the key pillars of the post-war international system) which provided the catalyst for the largely peaceful collapse of Europe's bipolar system.

It is important to recognise that the four secular trends noted above were part and parcel of a broader process of change in the wider international system. From the late 1950s onwards, the global bipolar order had begun to fragment, first with the emergence of the non-aligned movement, and then with the Sino-Soviet split. At the same time, the uneven nature of economic development resulted in new foci of economic activity (for example in East Asia or Latin America), along with a qualitative and quantitative growth in the level of world trade and international financial exchanges. This has gradually produced a more polycentric world order characterised by thickening webs of interdependence. The underlying cause for this change in the international system has been developments in the global economy, with the growing internationalisation of the world market and the development of new transnational modes of production, commerce and information exchange. These trends towards transnational integration and what has been termed 'complex interdependence' contributed towards the ultimate collapse of the bipolar order in Europe, and today are playing a decisive role in shaping the new, post-Cold War order on the continent.

BEYOND BIPOLARITY: EUROPE'S CHANGING TOPOLOGY

The collapse of the bipolar certainties of the Cold War era has been followed by a period of considerable flux in European politics. The ramifications of this have been experienced at many different levels – from the changing party political balance in Italy and Germany, to the changing structural dynamics of the European interstate system. The demise of the Cold War forced all the main multilateral organisations in Europe to rethink their purpose and rationale, and led to considerable soul-searching in the foreign and defence ministries of the main European powers. But already the outlines of a new European interstate system are beginning to emerge – and it is clear that the new Europe will be unique. The emerging European security system has no parallel elsewhere in the world, and no direct historical precedent in Europe itself. It is certainly very different from the Bismarckian balance of power system of the late nineteenth and early twentieth century, and very different from the Concert of Europe of Metternich's era. Although the precise contours of the new Europe are still somewhat hazy, it is now possible to identify the main features of this unique European system.

The first characteristic of the new Europe is its blurred edges. Of all the continents, the Eurasian landmass is the one with the most indistinct boundaries. Europe can be defined as the north-west corner of the Eurasian landmass, but this begs the question of where the precise cut-off point between Europe and Asia lies. In the absence of any clear geographical boundary, any definition of 'Europe' is bound to be an arbitrary one based on political criterion. Indeed, 'Europe', it has been argued, is 'not so much a place as an issue' (Buzan *et al.* 1990: 49). In the Medieval era, 'Europe' was equated with Christendom and the boundaries of the Carolingian Empire (which is roughly equivalent to the original EC six). Somewhat more idiosyncratically, Prince Metternich once declared that immediately across the Rennweg, the street which runs right through Vienna, one is already in the Balkans, and in Asia (Magris 1990: 241). Since then, the political concept of what constitutes Europe has expanded slowly eastwards and south-easterly. This has meant that at different times, Europe's eastern edge has been defined as the Danube, the Elbe, the Vistula or the Ural Mountains. Today, many commentators use the expression 'Europe from the Atlantic to the Urals', but even this raises some problems. For example, both Turkey and Russia straddle Europe and Asia. The break-up of the Soviet Union has added further complications: the central Asian republics have been admitted to the Conference on Security and Cooperation in Europe, whilst the Caucasian republics – Georgia, Armenia and Azerbaijan – may fall within the geographical area of Europe, but culturally, politically and economically, they have more in common with their neighbours in south-west Asia and the Middle East.

From this we can identify four basic concepts of what constitutes 'Europe'. The first is Europe as western Europe, particularly the European Community. This is apparently the concept of 'Europe' entertained by the east central Europeans when they speak of a 'return to Europe'. It is also a vision of Europe which has its historical antecedents in the ninth century Carolingian Empire. Secondly, a Europe 'from the Atlantic to the Urals', embracing the Russians west of the Urals mountains, but, most significantly, excluding the North Americans. This was a concept of Europe popular with General De Gaulle, and one also advanced at various times during the Cold War by the Soviets. The third is Europe 'from Poland to Portugal': this excludes both the Americans and the former Soviet Union, and was a vision of Europe popular amongst sections of the peace movement and on the nationalist right. Finally, there is the notion of Europe used in the Helsinki Conference on the Security and Cooperation in Europe (CSCE) protocols and documents, which speak of the 'European security area': this includes the North Americans, and – more recently – all the successor states to the former Soviet Union, even those in central Asia. Any definition of 'Europe', therefore, is inevitably a political one.

Each of the definitions advanced above has its strengths and its weaknesses. In the end, one has to recognise that the notion of 'Europe' is an abstract one, and that no precise and commonly agreed borders to Europe can be identified.

None the less, although Europe may lack distinct edges, it undoubtedly possesses an identifiable 'core'. It is this that provides the second key feature of the new Europe. The core of Europe is its north-western area, from southern England in the north to northern Italy in the south, and from France in the west to the Benelux countries and western Germany in the east. This area constitutes the core by virtue of its level of economic development, the intensity of its transnational social, economic and cultural exchanges, and the thickening webs of interdependence and cross-border integration that criss-cross the region. The region's economic centrality has been complemented and reinforced by its growing political cohesion, as the EC has both expanded its membership and deepened its political integration. Moreover, this region is implicitly acknowledged to be the core of the new Europe by countries to its south or east, all of whom seek to draw closer to it and to share in its prosperity and stability.

The third key feature of the new Europe is the re-emergence of distinct regional patterns of cooperation and conflict. The east–west conflict imposed a high degree of strategic unity on the continent. The existence of a commonly perceived external enemy in the shape of the Soviet Union and its Warsaw Pact allies, for example, united NATO countries as disparate as Norway and Turkey, and Greece and Denmark. Although as we have seen, regional factors qualified the dynamics of the east–west rivalry on the peripheries, throughout the continent the overwhelming security concern was the fear of a large-scale NATO–Warsaw Pact conflict.

The end of the Cold War has shattered this sense of strategic unity, and led to a fragmentation of the continent along regional lines. Today, the security concerns of a country like Norway (faced with the emergence of new democracies around the Baltic Sea, but with a substantial Russian military capability in the Kola Peninsula) are fundamentally different from those of its NATO ally Turkey (which borders on the Balkans, the Caucasus and the Middle East – all areas of considerable turbulent and violent conflict). In this sense, therefore, European security has become 'divisible', as Richard Ullman has argued (1991: 27–8). The nascent trends towards regionalism which were increasingly apparent from the 1960s onwards have thus become so strong that today they constitute one of the key features of the new Europe.

There are a number of distinct regional groupings, some of which have acquired an institutional expression. The Baltic, for example, constitutes a specific grouping of states which share a number of common economic, environmental, political and security concerns. Meetings of government leaders and parliamentarians from Nordic and Baltic countries have taken place, which has led to the creation of a Baltic Sea Cooperation Council in March 1992. The three east-central European countries (Poland, Czechoslovakia and Hungary) also share common economic, political and strategic concerns, and on 17 April 1992 established a central European Cooperation Committee in Budapest. The main focus of this body is economic cooperation, the aim being to establish a free trade zone and to coordinate their policies towards the EC. A third regional organisation, one established in the immediate wake of the ending of the Cold War, was the Pentagonale. This consisted of Italy, Austria, Hungary, Czechoslovakia and Yugoslavia – the old *Mitteleuropaeischer* lands of the former Habsburg Empire. The Pentagonale became the Hexagonale in the summer of 1991 with the accession of Poland, although since then the effectiveness of this body has been reduced given the civil war in former Yugoslavia. None the less, various forms of cooperation in south-central Europe will undoubtedly continue, given the strong demand for it in the region.

Two other areas with a strong regional identity are southern Europe and the Balkans. The Mediterranean countries of southern Europe share common economic, environmental and security problems. Spain, Portugal, France and Italy are all concerned about the danger of a large-scale influx of economically motivated refugees coming from the north African littoral, and have consequently begun coordinating their security policies in the western Mediterranean. Many of them also constitute the poorer members of the EC, and, in cooperation with other less prosperous countries on the periphery of the EC's north-western core (namely Ireland and Greece), are campaigning for Community funds to be diverted to their economies to facilitate a process of 'levelling up'.

The Balkans is another area where regionalisation is under way. The Balkans is traditionally a very distinctive region where politics and international relations have their own discrete logic and dynamic. Although it is currently the elements of discord and conflict which are most in evidence as a consequence of the violent break-up of the Yugoslav Federation, there have over recent years been heartening signs of cooperation. Beginning in February 1988, a series of meetings have taken place between the foreign ministers of the six Balkan countries, and attempts have been made to find collaborative solutions to shared problems. The substantive results to date have been modest; but the very fact that such attempts at regional cooperation have been made in the recent past gives some hope that the problems stemming from the Yugoslavia crisis will not trigger off wider conflicts in this region – a region once dubbed 'the powder-keg of Europe'. Chris Cviic has also argued that 'regional groupings are likely to assume an ever greater importance in Europe during the rest of the 1990s and beyond', and has suggested two possibilities for regional integration in south-eastern Europe: a *Kleinmitteleuropa* (Little Central Europe) of Austria, Bosnia, former Czechoslovakia, Croatia, Hungary and Slovenia; and a Balkan confederation (which he dubs '*Balkania*'), grouping together the Orthodox countries of Bulgaria, Greece, Montenegro, Romania, Serbia and possibly an independent Macedonia (Cviic 1991: 104–5).

The emerging regionalisation of Europe underlines how far the politics in the continent have developed since the bipolar days of the Cold War. The new Europe is in many ways an exciting mix of old and new. The new regional patterns of cooperation mentioned above result from the greater interdependence and integration on the continent; as economic activity has become increasingly transnational, political cooperation has been institutionalised, and socio-cultural interaction has become more intensive. In this sense, the growing awareness of regional identity is a very modern development. Yet it is also the product of deep-seated cultural, economic and political ties which have their roots deep within the centuries-old history of Europe. Baltic cooperation, for example, harks back to the former Hanseatic League, whilst the Hexagonale explicitly draws upon a romanticised picture of the old Habsburg Empire – once described as the 'prison-house of nations', but now seen in some quarters as an enviable example of multinational coexistence and cooperation. In form, therefore, the new patterns of regional cooperation are deeply historical and traditional; in substance, however, they are the product of the more modern forces of transnational interdependence and international integration which have transformed the nature of European politics in the late twentieth century.

THE INSTITUTIONAL 'ARCHITECTURE' OF THE NEW EUROPE

Economic and political forces at work within any international system tend to give rise to specific institutional structures. At the same time, institutional structures can play an important role in channelling – and to some extent shaping – the direction and effectiveness of these elemental forces. The relationship between economic and political forces and institutions is thus a 'dialectical' one, in that they interact in complex ways one upon the other. For example, the establishment of the EC in 1957 was a response to the growth in transnational economic activity and a desire for institutionalised political cooperation; at the same time, the existence of the Community has helped accelerate the deepening economic integration and political cohesion amongst its member states.

In Europe's new institutional architecture, the EC, NATO and the CSCE will play vital roles. Although other organisations – such as the Council of Europe, the Western European Union (WEU) and the European Bank for Reconstruction and Development (EBRD) – may well grow in importance, it is these three bodies which will predominate. The relationship between these three, therefore, will decisively influence the character of the institutional dynamics in the new Europe.

Of the three, it is undoubtedly the EC which is the single most important organisation. If, as has already been argued, the geo-economic core of the post-Cold War Europe is its north-west region, then its institutional core is the EC. It provides a focus for economic integration in Europe, for growing political cohesion and attracts non-members to its club. The Community is also broadening its range of competences away from its traditional focus on economic and trade policy, and is now developing a common foreign and security policy. It is thus the EC which, more than any other single body, embodies the spirit of the new Europe, with its aspirations for a continent economically prosperous, politically cohesive and at peace with itself and its neighbours.

Whilst the disintegration of the bipolar system has left the EC as Europe's key organisation, it has not as yet led to the collapse of NATO as some had envisaged. During the armed stand-off of the Cold War years, NATO was vital to the security of western Europe, and provided a protective umbrella under which the EC could flourish. But as an organisation designed, in the words of its first Secretary-General Lord Ismay, to 'keep the Russians out, the Americans in and the Germans down', some analysts expected that the Alliance would inevitably become redundant following the end of the Cold War. This, however, has not yet happened, and reports of the imminent demise of the Alliance seem premature. NATO has undoubtedly declined in importance relative to the EC, particularly given that the fear which led to its creation – namely of a large-scale east–west conflict – looks increasingly unlikely. None the less, it is likely to continue to play an important role for three main reasons. First, because it institutionalises a permanent US commitment to the continent, which most European governments see as a stabilising factor. Secondly, it provides an insurance policy for the west Europeans in the event of a recidivist set-back to the reform programme in the former Soviet Union. Thirdly, because it provides a framework for institutionalised multilateral military cooperation amongst its sixteen member states. In the light of Europe's fractious past, this multilateral cooperation enjoys wide support as an antidote to the risk of a 'renationalisation' of defence policy in western Europe.

Whilst the EC has grown in stature, and NATO has preserved a significant role for itself in the post-Cold War system, it is the CSCE which represents the real success story of modern European diplomacy at the systemic level. From being a mere 'process' designed to ameliorate the worst excesses of the east–west conflict, the CSCE has now become a permanent institutionalised fixture in the new European architecture, with a pan-European composition and comprehensive issue-agenda. The seminal point for the post-Cold War CSCE was the Meeting of CSCE Heads of State and Government held in Paris in November 1990. It was this summit which issued the 'Paris Charter for a New Europe' and which inaugerated the 'institutionalisation' of the CSCE. Since then, the CSCE has acquired a permanent Secretariat in Prague; a Conflict Prevention Centre in Vienna; an Office of Free Elections in Warsaw; a parliamentary Assembly; regular, six-monthly meetings of a newly created 'Council of Foreign Ministers'; regular meetings of a 'Committee of Senior Officials'; and CSCE summit meetings once every two years. At the same time, the CSCE has acquired new procedures for monitoring 'unusual military activity' and human rights violations, and an 'Emergency Mechanism' for convening meetings to discuss problems of common concern falling within the remit of the CSCE. These new procedures and emergency mechanisms have to a significant extent modified the previous principle of unanimous decision-making. At the same time, the CSCE has grown in size as it has accepted new member states from the former USSR and Yugoslavia, and now embraces virtually all the states in Europe (from Vancouver to Vladivostock).

Thus although the CSCE lacks effective mechanisms for crisis management and conflict resolution (and can therefore not as yet provide a suitable instrument for a pan-European collective security regime), it does have an important role to play on the systemic level. First, it can provide a forum for rule-setting and the elaboration of commonly agreed political principles within the European interstate system. Secondly, it provides a mechanism for monitoring and judging the actions of governments by their peers, on the basis of the mutually agreed normative framework. In this way, the CSCE may be able to act as the 'collective conscience' of the new Europe.

These three multilateral organisations, therefore, will be decisive in shaping the structural dynamics of Europe's new architecture. Already they are beginning to interact in interesting and innovative ways. For example, the CSCE provided pan-European endorsement for the diplomatic initiatives of the EC during the Yugoslav civil war (Salmon 1992: 229). It has also been agreed in principle that NATO could in future provide military forces for peace-keeping operations sanctioned by the CSCE (*Financial Times*, 22.5.92). At the same time other institutional links are being built between these three organisations: for example, the WEU is widely regarded as a potential 'bridge' between the North Atlantic Alliance and the European Community, whilst the Council of Europe provides a link between the work of the CSCE and that of the Community in the sphere of human rights.

The new architecture of Europe will therefore be characterised by considerable institutional pluralism, along with a high degree of functional diversity. Thus, for example, whilst the EC will provide the focus for economic and political integration, matters of military security will tend to remain the preserve of NATO, with the WEU playing a complementary role. Meanwhile, the CSCE will provide a forum for pan-European dialogue and cooperation, and the Council of Europe will concern itself with the legal dimension of human rights. The evolving international system in Europe will thus comprise a pluralistic institutional ensemble comprising a number of interlocking and overlapping structures. This will involve a complex web of multilateral organisations, alliances, international economic organisations, regional organisations and a network of bi- and multilateral relationships. In this multi-layered structure, international functions and responsibilities will be distributed between different bodies and through different levels. Such a rich diversity of different organisations and institutions will correspond to the heterogeneity of Europe, its blurred edges, its varied historical experiences and its diverse economic and political requirements (Hyde-Price 1991: 250–2).

THE NEW DYNAMICS OF STATE-BUILDING AND ETHNO-NATIONAL CONFLICT

Undoubtedly the crucial question that the demise of the Cold War poses for Europe today is whether it will lead to a continent more or less integrated, and more or less peaceful? What, in other words, are the implications of the end of the east–west conflict for the stability and security of the continent? When the Cold War came to an end in the late 1980s, there was initially an up-beat mood of optimism. Many people hoped that for the first time ever there was a realistic possibility of achieving what the Germans called a 'European peace order' (*europäisiche Friedensordnung*), or what President Bush referred to as a continent 'whole and free'. A few years on from the *annus mirabilis* of 1989, however, the mood of optimism has been replaced by a deepening sense of foreboding. Many people now fear that the relative stability and predictability of the Cold War is being replaced by a resurgence of national rivalries and inter-ethnic conflicts across Europe. They fear that in the absence of a common unifying external threat, traditional animosities and deep-seated tensions will re-emerge, bringing war to parts of the post-communist world, and threatening the stability and prosperity of western Europe.

In the same way as the optimism which accompanied the 1989 events was overblown, the current tendency towards pessimism is also misplaced. It is certainly the case that nationalism, along with religion, has re-emerged as a powerful political force in the post-communist world. However, it has re-emerged in the context of a continent transformed by thickening networks of interdependence and transnational integration. As Hans-Dietrich Genscher has noted:

> Through the political integration of Western Europe, traditional sources of conflict have been put aside. They have been replaced by a growing European awareness of interdependent interests. The national conflicts and uncertainties caused by the collapse of communism in Eastern and South-Eastern Europe have not spread. This is a positive result of post-war political developments in Western Europe, which must not be underestimated.

> (Genscher 1992)

The attractive pull of the EC and the desire of many of the new democracies in central and eastern Europe to move closer to the economic core of the continent also gives the EC leverage to encourage a peaceful resolution of disputes. This has helped ameliorate some of the ethno-national tensions in east-central Europe. Even where this is of limited impact, as has been the case for example in former Yugoslavia, the picture is not one of unremitting bleakness, for as Chris Cviic has argued:

> the really new – and, for all those interested in the area, exciting – thing is that, for the first time in their recent history, the people of the Balkans seem to be on their own, with no external powers trying to impose their will either on the region as a whole, or on any parts of it. The upheavals that are taking place there (and the attendant instability) are not being caused by external forces, as always happened in the past, but are occurring as a result of pressure from within, exerted by indigenous forces.

> (Cviic 1991: 1)

Europe today, therefore, has not as a whole reverted to the nationalist rivalries and balance of power politics of the nineteenth and early twentieth centuries. Moreover, one of the distinguishing characteristics of European politics in the 1990s is the absence of a major 'rogue' power. This contrasts starkly with the interwar years, when attempts to establish a system of collective security based on the League of Nations foundered because of the rogue behaviour of fascist Italy, Nazi Germany and Stalinist Russia. To some extent, therefore, the post-Cold War Europe embodies elements of a new 'Concert of Europe', comparable to the Concert system of Metternich in the years from 1815–53. There is a pronounced tendency amongst the major powers in Europe to identify areas of consensus and agreement between them in order to find cooperative solutions to common problems. This has been accompanied by a greater respect for international law, and a much greater commitment to both collaborative diplomacy and concerted action to prevent substantial violations of commonly accepted norms of international behaviour. The current European 'concert' differs from its nineteenth-century predecessor however, in that it is not being exercised to prevent the democratic right to national self-determination, nor against the interest of the smaller powers.

There is thus good reason for believing that the overall security environment in the continent has improved as a consequence of the end of the Cold War. This is particularly the case in central Europe, where forty years of military confrontation is steadily being dismantled. Nevertheless, there are new challenges to the security and stability of Europe arising from the changed dynamics of nation-building and the disintegration of states. Since the rise of modern nationalism at the time of the Great French Revolution of 1789, the process of nation-state building has rarely been peaceful. The unifications of Germany and Italy were accompanied by wars, whilst the break-up of the Ottoman, Habsburg and Tsarist Empires were the consequence of the First World War. During the Cold War, nationalist pressures in central and eastern Europe were largely contained by the wider pressures of the east–west conflict. The demise of the Cold War, however, has seen the process of nation-building and the disintegration of multinational states resuming – for example, Germany and former Yugoslavia. The impact of new republics on the European state system is difficult to assess. As one American analyst has written:

> It is important to recognize that the very existence of states creates certain dynamics for their immediate neighbours and for the continent as a whole. However, analyzing the potential ramifications remains difficult. For some nations – a united Germany, the former Warsaw pact nations, and even the Baltics for a brief period – there is some historical

record to draw upon in assessing how their independent existence will affect European dynamics. However, for other states – primarily Ukraine, but potentially Byelorussia and the Caucasian republics, and Slovenia – there are no precedents upon which to draw for their likely behaviour or their effect on the European state system.

(Lowenthal 1991: 3)

The new European system therefore does not correspond to any previous structure of international relations in Europe. Rather, it comprises a unique blend of a number of different 'models' (or 'ideal types') of international relations: to begin with, in western Europe a 'pluralist security community' has developed; this means that armed conflict between the members of this community of states is simply inconceivable. Secondly, a new 'Concert of Europe' between the Great Powers seems to have emerged, reminiscent in some respects of the age of Metternich. Thirdly, the new mechanisms for conflict prevention and crisis management within the recently institutionalised CSCE framework seem to provide the embryonic structures for a system of pan-European collective security, similar in some ways to the League of Nations. Finally, however, in eastern Europe, the former Soviet Union and the Balkans, a more traditional balance of power system is taking shape, as the new republics manoeuvre to achieve military security and political advantage over their neighbours and rivals, in an area riddled with disputed borders, minority groups and nationalist irredentia.

CONCLUSION: TOWARDS A EUROPE 'WHOLE AND FREE'?

From the analysis presented above, it can be seen that on a systemic level, the most important structural dynamic in the Europe of the 1990s is the dialectic between the stability, relative prosperity and growing integration of Europe's north-western core, and the fragmentation, nationalist discord and economic crisis of the former communist lands to its east. It is this interaction between the western and eastern parts of the continent which gives European international relations its unique flavour in the post-Cold War era.

This means that the central task facing Europeans today is overcoming the legacy of the east–west conflict, and building a more united, democratic and peaceful Europe – a Europe 'whole and free'. This is a major task which will occupy the talents of the continent's political and economic elites for a generation or more. Already, as Hans-Dietrich Genscher has argued, the process of growing together has already begun:

> It is taking place within a series of complementary frameworks: the European Community, NATO, the Conference on Security and Co-operation in Europe (CSCE), the Council of Europe, the North Atlantic Cooperation Council and the Western European Union.

> The European Community and the Western Alliance are the cores from which Europe can draw strength. These institutions must be further and decisively developed – both internally and externally.

> (Genscher 1992)

All the main European organisations are now developing or strengthening their pan-European dimension. The EC is actively considering the implications of the 'widening' of the Community to include new members from both the European Free Trade Area (EFTA) countries and from the new democracies of central and eastern Europe (Gnesotto 1992). Indeed, this was a major concern of the British Presidency of the Community in the second half of 1992. Similarly, NATO has established a new forum for institutionalising dialogue and consultation with its former adversaries in the Warsaw Pact – the 'North Atlantic Cooperation Council' (NACC). The NACC was inaugurated in Brussels on 20 December 1991, and now contains thirty-six members: NATO's sixteen members, five former Warsaw Pact member states, the three Baltic republics, eleven Commonwealth of Independent States (CIS) members and Georgia. The Council of Europe has also accepted some of the new democracies as members, whilst the WEU is also actively developing its contacts with these states. The aim of all these endeavours is to try to draw the countries of central and eastern Europe into a deepening network of economic interdependence and institutionalised multilateral cooperation. In this way, it is hoped gradually to extend the 'pluralistic security community' of western Europe eastwards to include more and more of the former communist world.

What, then, are the structural requirements of this new, post-Cold War European system? Stanley Hoffmann once wrote that all political systems must fulfil three conditions, 'security, satisfaction, and flexibility' (Hoffmann 1965: 20). If the new European system is to meet these conditions, it must develop an institutional architecture based on complementarity between Europe's key organisations, particularly the EC, NATO and the CSCE. It also requires the refining of new mechanisms for managing conflict and international dissension: this is vital because it is impossible to eradicate all sources of tension and instability from the continent (especially those associated with deep-seated ethno-national animosities). Instead, new instruments for crisis prevention and conflict management must be developed, primarily within the framework of the CSCE, but also involving the EC, the NACC and the United Nations. Moreover, it is vital that collective, multilateral structures for managing Europe's security problems be developed, in order to spread the burden and responsibilities these problems will generate. Otherwise there is a danger that Germany will be left to bear the load of supporting economic and political change in central and eastern Europe. This risks overloading a Germany already suffering from severe domestic problems (arising from the costs of unification) and unsure of its international role. Finally, in seeking to give shape to the new European system of international relations, we should act as 'gardeners and not mechanics', to use the apt expression of George Kennan (Matthews *et al.* 1989: 451). In other words, we must recognise that the post-Cold War system in Europe will not be the product of any conscious architectural plan or grand scheme, but will evolve gradually in an organic manner, in response to specific crises and challenges. Metaphorically speaking, therefore, the new Europe will be more like a jazz combo (with substantial scope for creative improvisation within a loose arrangement) rather than a traditional orchestra following the disciplined instructions of a conductor's baton.

NOTES

1   The observations of Max Planck are as valid for the study of international relations as they are for modern physics: 'In physics . . . we regard all complicated processes as combinations of simple elementary processes . . . that is, we think of the wholes before us as the sum of their parts. But this procedure presupposes that the splitting of a whole does not affect the character of this whole . . . One cannot understand such processes on the assumption that all properties of a whole may be approached by a study of its parts' (quoted in Gillette and Frank 1990: 63).

2   'There are now two great nations in the world which, starting from different points, seem to be advancing towards the same goal: the Russians and the Anglo-Americans.

   Both have grown in obscurity, and while the world's attention was occupied elsewhere, they have suddenly taken their place among the leading nations, making the world take note of their birth and of their greatness almost at the same instant . . .

   Their point of departure is different and their paths diverse: nevertheless, each seems called by some secret design of Providence one day to hold in its hands the destinies of half the world' (Alexis de Tocqueville, *Democracy in America*, 1863).

Chapter 3

The state level

The nation-state in Europe, east and west
David Sadler

In many ways the state has been the subject in focus as the dramatic political events in Europe have unfolded in recent years. In eastern and central Europe, the various states of the Soviet bloc successively threw off the shackles of Soviet hegemony in the revolutions of 1989. Although the new regimes were immediately confronted with chronic economic realities, which have barely eased today, for the first time in over 40 years the leaders of these states were, theoretically at least, masters of their own destinies – free to fashion their own economic, social and political systems and able to pursue a 'normal' or independent path in international relations.[1]

An important causal factor in the revolutions of 1989 was the search for national identity in contrast to an imposed and bankrupt ideology, which was a thin veil for Soviet domination. The nationalist tide in eastern and central Europe has continued, however. Ethnic conflicts now further threaten the stability of these ex-communist regimes. Nationalism unsettled then toppled the multinational states of the USSR and Yugoslavia in 1991. Out of the disintegration of these states new nation-states, often recalling great independent histories, have emerged, also plagued by economic collapse, religious strife and ethnic conflicts to varying degrees. Thus a period of state-building has begun in the east, but in very difficult circumstances. One manifestation of these changes is the significant numerical expansion in the number of legally independent, sovereign states in Europe. Fifty-two states were represented at the July 1992 (CSCE) Conference in Helsinki compared to a membership of thirty-five which existed during the greater part of the CSCE's history.[2]

The current position is far from stable with separatist forces gathering strength in many places. Czechoslovakia has experienced a bitter divorce just three years after the 'velvet revolution'. Separatist violence has flared in Moldova, Georgia and in other parts of the region. Traditional prejudices, fears and animosities have reappeared after decades of cold storage under communist rule. A full-scale civil war in parts of former Yugoslavia now rages, with increasing evidence of genocidal practices. As one commentator has noted, the current instability is multi-faceted but driven by the profound economic crisis throughout the region:

> The ex-communist states' threat to the stability of Eastern and Central Europe and to international security can be traced to two basic sources: one concerning ethnic, religious and national relationships, the other springing from the fact that political, social and economic transformations are taking place in conditions of a profound crisis. Both these sources are strongly intertwined. The visible growth of nationalism, ethnic tensions, interstate conflicts and those related to the dissolution of the USSR and Yugoslavia are, to a considerable degree, the result of the search for a way out of the economic collapse.
>
> (Smolar 1992: 27)

The new states have chosen to internally organise their polities in increasingly different and diverse ways. Some have moved further towards political reform whilst others continue to display authoritarian tendencies. Almost everywhere there is at least the rhetoric of radical economic reform in the direction of a market economy, but the practice reveals great differences. Everywhere there is a growing realisation of the magnitude of the task and a fear of the social consequences. Poland and Hungary are two states who have attempted to make the painful adjustments; whereas the process has hardly begun in the Ukraine, for example.

The process of economic and political reform is requiring an ongoing debate about the role of the state. After decades of stultifying statism, there is clearly a need for civic society to be allowed room to develop. But paradoxically, if the economic reforms are to be successfully pursued then the state in eastern Europe will continue to play a shaping role, if only until a successful market economy is established.

By contrast to all this upheaval and instability in the east, the western states appear relatively stable. Their social, political and economic systems are not in question, at least in their fundamentals. Centrifugal tensions do exist, but these have been contained without challenge to the overall integrity of western states.

One of the more remarkable trends in western Europe in recent years has been the accelerated drive towards European integration. The 1986 Single European Act has unblocked much of the paralysis in EC decision-making. It sets in train the '1992 process' which will greatly liberalise Community markets when fully implemented. The Maastricht Treaty, if ratified, will advance European integration through its two major components: economic and monetary union (EMU) and political union. These and other developments have provoked considerable political and academic speculation on the future of the state in the EC.[3] Concerns over the loss of national sovereignty to supranational institutions and the capacity for independent national action, in conjunction with other issues such as immigration, account for a great deal of the ratification difficulties the Maastricht Treaty has suffered in Denmark and will potentially suffer elsewhere.[4]

Despite these controversies, the EC continues to exercise a magnetic attraction to the states of Europe. The Community has gone through successive enlargements since its creation in 1957. Further enlargements are likely by 1995/1996 with the entry of many of the EFTA countries, to be followed at a later date by consideration of east European states. Fears of being marginalised and a recognition of the economic benefits of membership lie behind much of the attractiveness of the Community to states, despite the restrictions on the exclusive power of national decision-making that membership entails in an increasing number of fields. Although the path to greater integration has not been one which has been consistently followed throughout the history of the Community, with states keen to preserve their powers *vis-à-vis* the supranational organs, the scope of the Community in the affairs of states has inexorably grown.[5] Despite the often bitter disputes between Community members, withdrawal is not a serious option for any existing member. The EC has also played a significant role in developing a web of relations between states that makes war between them dysfunctional and now unthinkable.

Another driving force behind integration efforts would appear to be German unification. Germany is of immense importance in Europe because of the strength and direction its economy offers to the Community and to Europe more widely. This is reinforced by Germany's geographical proximity to central and eastern Europe. An article in *The Economist* stated:

> It is easy to forget how, when the Berlin Wall ruptured in 1989, there were fears that Germany would drift into no-man's land in its search for national unity, watering down its commitment to the EC and NATO . . . [then in 1990] First Helmut Kohl, the German Chancellor, then François Mitterand, the French President, were seized by an urge to swaddle Germany in European obligations before the re-united country could develop other instincts.
>
> (*The Economist*, 1992f)

How then should we characterise the trends in both east and west? One perspective suggests that eastern Europe, especially the Balkans, is 'going back in history', by contrast, western Europe is moving, by evolutionary process, to a novel form of political organisation (Smolar 1992: 27). Thus:

> two diametrically opposed trends are apparent: while Western Europe is moving towards greater integration and multilateral cooperation, eastern Europe is becoming entangled in a spiral of increasing fragmentation and 'renationalisation' of politics.
>
> (Smolar 1992: 27)

Another analysis suggests although the process in east and west is different, the result, at least for some eastern states, is much the same:

> It is the fate of many existing nation-states to have their sovereignty eroded from above and below, that is, from the pressures of supranational economic integration and from new sub-nationalisms that will suddenly appear.
>
> (Fukuyama 1992: 23)

Both perspectives appear to be based on a number of assumptions which will be tested. First, the assumption is of an increased threat to the existence of the nation-state in western Europe as integration proceeds. Certainly membership of the EC entails some loss of national sovereignty, but it is not as yet total. There are a range of arguments which point to the continued centrality of the state and these are discussed later. Secondly, although all eastern European states face acute economic problems, it has to be proven that they are all vulnerable to the centrifugal forces of ethnic conflict and subnationalism.

A distinguishing feature of the post-Cold War Europe is the complex diversity and hierarchy of states. At one extreme stands Albania, re-emerging after years of grim isolation. One influential survey terms it 'the Invalid State' (IISS 1992: 41) with a significant proportion of its population seeking to flee to neighbouring countries as communist economic structures collapse without any discernible or effective programmes to replace them. Bosnia – Hercegovina represents another state existing in quite the grimmest of circumstances with every prospect of enforced partition as a result of the military successes of the Bosnian Serbs. At the other extreme stands Germany, which despite the enormous strains of unification, retains the strongest economy in Europe. Generally, the disparity between the economic fortunes of the ex-communist states compared to those in western Europe impart a new dimension to east–west relations with one observer warning of a 'European Rio Grande' with the lines of division forming around the issues of unemployment, immigration, debt, inflation and political instability (Smolar 1992: 26).

The power hierarchy in Europe has become magnified by the combination of the emergence of new states, the collapse of communism and the unification of Germany. The Cold War imposed a degree of discipline on the behaviour of states,[6] or at least those within the respective blocs. Now that the Cold War has passed into history, power relationships may become more salient.

A POWER HIERARCHY?

Europe has witnessed a growth in the number of legally independent sovereign states. Sovereignty has, as Northedge notes:

> an internal and external connotation. Internally, it generally means supreme competence to make law within the determined frontiers of the state to the exclusion of any other law-making authorities . . . Externally, however, sovereignty does not mean 'supremacy', but 'equality' . . . A sovereign state, then, is nothing more nor less than an entity which participates in the international system on a level of legal or formal equality with all such similar members of the system.
>
> (Northedge 1976: 142–3)

The voluntary transfer of sovereignty to the supranational institutions of the EC obviously raises complications with respect to the sovereign status of the member states under this definition. For the moment, however, we will concentrate on the external aspect of sovereignty. Sovereignty under this formulation is essentially a legal concept. It does not describe how the sovereign state will fare in the international arena. The success or otherwise of any state's attempt to further its interests depends upon the power it possesses. Power in turn derives from the ability to mobilise various tangible and intangible resources.[7] Tangible resources include economic and military power. Political power can derive from intangible and tangible resources, including recognition of sovereign status by other states, membership of international organisations, diplomatic prowess or charismatic leadership as well as the possession of economic and/or military power.

The identification of a single power hierarchy of states in Europe is difficult because European states possess varying amounts of the resources which comprise power. Globally only the USA still possesses a sufficient range and depth of the resources necessary to be considered a superpower.

Economic power is concentrated in the states of western Europe, especially in the countries of the north-west. With gross domestic product (GDP) per capita significantly above the EC average in 1990, Norway,

Sweden, Finland and Switzerland must be added to this list (*The Economist* 1992b). The most significant economic power in Europe is clearly Germany. As the real cost of unification sinks in, indicators point to increased economic difficulties. German interest rates have risen in response to rising inflation and taxation rates have increased to finance the reconstruction of the east. For similar reasons the current account balance went into deficit in 1991 for the first time in a decade. German public sector debt, while still under the Group of Seven (G7 – the seven leading industrial powers) average of 60 per cent of GNP, is rising and may top 51 per cent by 1994 if public spending continues at current rates (*The Economist* 1992c). In the eastern sector of Germany considerable disenchantment has developed. Unemployment rates are rising as the inefficient industries of the east are privatised or go bankrupt. But anxiety about the state of the economy is burnt into the German psyche (Marsh 1989: 119–47). Over the longer term there are reasons to believe that eastern Germany will possess one of the most competitive and modern economies in Europe. The Deutschmark still acts as the lynchpin of the Exchange Rate Mechanism. The collapse of COMECON has handed Germany the role of the leading trade partner of the majority of the states of eastern and central Europe.

In military terms there are a number of more significant actors than Germany, however. Russia possesses the largest military forces on the continent, with significant capability in both conventional weaponry and weapons of mass destruction, even after negotiated and unilateral reductions. Ukraine, the size of France, has assembled one of the largest standing armies in Europe, although it plans to reduce significantly the 500,000 men currently under arms. While this force is of more concern to Ukraine's immediate neighbours, western states will keep a careful watch on Ukrainian adherence to their pledges on the tactical and strategic nuclear weapons on their soil, which are slated for removal and destruction by 1994.

Britain and France are also more important militarily than Germany. Unlike Germany, they are nuclear weapon states. They possess conventional forces of some significance and retain independent and collaborative production capabilities in many key sectors. British and French forces also have significant experience of out-of-area engagements. Germany by contrast is not a nuclear weapon state. The Basic Law does not permit German forces to operate outside German territory. Germany does possess considerable conventional forces, integrated into North Atlantic Treaty Organisation (NATO) structures, but these are currently being cut back considerably. The strategic importance of Germany has declined with the end of the Cold War confrontation of forces along the inner German border.

In political terms the situation is still more complex. Britain, France and Russia are permanent members of the United Nations Security Council and have thus played key roles in many important political decisions, not least the Security Council debates on Iraq since August 1990. Britain, France, Germany and Italy are also members of the G7. After the skill and bravery Yeltsin displayed during the August coup of 1991, the Russian President commands considerable personal power, which is made all the greater by recognition of the latent potential of the country he presides over. Germany clearly possesses considerable political power by virtue of its economic position and leading role within the EC. The centrality of its geographical location and the size of its population, at around 80 million, also make Germany of inescapable importance. Germany has long been encouraged to take a more active international role. It attracted criticism when it failed to do so during the Gulf War. Equally, however, worries surfaced when Germany pushed for the EC to recognise Slovenia and Croatia in 1991, despite the reservations of several member states. This schizophrenia on the part of the international community serves as a practical limitation on German power.

Whilst it is clear therefore that no single power hierarchy exists, there are great and growing disparities in the power of states on the continent. Meanwhile, the ongoing economic, political and ethnic crisis in central and eastern Europe is sapping the strength of the countries of this region.

PROBLEMS IN EASTERN EUROPE

At the economic level the problems the various states of the region face are similar. Privatisation of the thousands of inefficient state enterprises has brought or threatens sharp rises in unemployment. Production has fallen, with the World Bank predicting production per capita may not return to 1989 levels until 1996 (IISS 1992: 29). The collapse of COMECON and the Soviet market has wiped out traditional export markets. In 1991 the east European economies shrank by approximately 10 per cent in 1991 and by 20 per cent in Bulgaria. With the abandonment of price controls, inflation has become a serious factor, peaking at 400 per cent in Bulgaria in 1991.

Responses to this have been varied. Poland, former Czechoslovakia and Hungary have attracted the greatest attention in the west as the most adventurous reformers. Former Czechoslovakia launched a mass privatisation scheme in May 1992. The inevitable closures and job losses that immediately follow privatisations exacerbated the tension with Slovakia, where resistance to a sweeping introduction of market mechanisms is greater. Poland also introduced sweeping changes in 1990 by savagely cutting back public expenditure and making the zloty a convertible currency. But Poland is an example of the dangers of hasty reform: public unrest at the effect of these changes has caused a slowing of the economic tempo and privatisation of the inefficient state-owned enterprises has been interrupted. Hungary increased its hard currency exports by 41 per cent in 1991 and received about half of $1.5 bn foreign capital earmarked for eastern Europe and the former Soviet Union (IISS 1992: 29). But Hungary has not attempted to privatise the bulk of its state-owned enterprises. These remain an inefficient and inflationary drain on the Hungarian economy.

These countries have turned their hopes to greater trade with and eventual membership of the EC. Acting in unison through the Visegrad pact of 1991 they jointly negotiated association agreements with the EC which established the principle of a free trade area between the signatories. They hope that these agreements will also provide a foundation for subsequent Community membership and they were successful in inserting a statement to that effect in the Preamble to the agreements.

But it is clear that the transition to a market economy is proving more difficult for all the ex-communist states, with greater attendant political and social problems than may have appeared possible in 1989:

> The building of democratic systems and the transition to market economies in the countries of Central and Eastern Europe are affected by more impediments than were originally expected and the unholy legacy these countries have to deal with goes deeper and has wider ramifications than anyone could imagine.
>
> (Havel 1991)

The states are plagued by 'expectation gaps' when performance does not match up to the heady dreams which inspired the upheavals of 1989. The weakness of social forces essential for a successful infusion of market mechanisms has led to a need for the state to play an active role, despite the legacy of statism from forty years of communism. Thus 'the state then implements privatisation schemes, backs local self government, fosters the establishment of associations, trade unions and so on' (Smolar 1992: 30). Yet the state may not be up to this leading role, especially in times of acute crisis. In several countries the civil service has proved to be a formidable obstacle to reform. The political elites, drawn into power suddenly in 1989, may lack the expertise necessary to confront and remedy these problems.

Confounding further the hopes for eastern Europe are a series of interconnected and profound political crises. The shocks of the transition to a market economy have caused political repercussions in several countries. Poland has seen a wave of strikes in response to rising prices and declining living standards. The Polish Parliament is fragmented by the existence of twenty-nine separate political parties. One danger is a return to authoritarianism through the suspension of the constitution. Romanian miners brought violence to the streets of Bucharest in 1991 and there were a series of strikes in other sectors.

Political tensions in former Czechoslovakia led to the division of Czech and Slovak lands. This in turn raises the prospect of further tension between the Slovaks and the ethnic Hungarians that form 11 per cent of the population of Slovakia. Hungarian minorities in Romania and former Yugoslavia continue to be a source of tension between Budapest and these countries.

The question of ethnic minorities threatens the integrity of several states in the region and is already a cause of major disorder in Bosnia–Hercegovina and Croatia. Georgia is facing violent insurrection from rebels in Abkhazia and South Ossetia. The Russian 14th Army has intervened on behalf of Russian-speaking rebel forces in Moldova, which itself is developing ever closer links with Romania. The last two examples highlight the problem of ethnic Russian minorities. Over eleven million Russians live in the Ukraine, comprising 22 per cent of the population. This problem is closely interrelated to the Russian claim over the Crimea, which the Ukraine controls. The two states are further at odds over control of the Black Sea Fleet. In Latvia and Estonia, Russians form over 30 per cent of the local population.

This question is a problem in several ways. The presence of substantial numbers of ethnic minorities complicates nation-building and is a source of friction in periods of economic crisis and nationalist resurgence. In the June 1992 referendum in Estonia voting was limited to those who had lived in the republic in 1938 or their descendants. This ensured the exclusion of the Russian-speaking minority who largely arrived in Estonia after 1940. In many countries laws require a knowledge of the local language for citizenship or government office. The once privileged Russian minorities are now experiencing serious disadvantage.

The response of Russian leaders will be crucial. An increasing number argue that Russia should make itself responsible for Russians everywhere. Vice-President Rutskoi warned of 'the inevitability of punishment' to states that suppress Russians. This was hours before the 14th Army intervened in Moldova.

The disintegration of Yugoslavia raises further ethnic problems (see

Chapter 8). Greece has protested at the use of the name Macedonia, fearing an independent Macedonia may have claims on the Macedonian region of Northern Greece. Bulgaria's swift recognition of Macedonia has worsened relations with Athens. The Serbian treatment of Albanians in the province of Kosovo is likely to be an additional source of tension in the Balkans.

This re-emergence of ethnic politics bears out the claim that eastern Europe is undergoing a renationalisation of politics. But the problems are more acute in the Balkans and in the republics of the former Soviet Union than central Europe, although former Czechoslovakia demonstrates that tensions exist there as well.

Having now outlined the trends in east European politics it is time to consider whether trends in the west display any similarities or diverge significantly.

THE STATE IN WESTERN EUROPE

Western Europe is not free of the rising tide of nationalism. In Germany the growth of nationalist and anti-immigrant sentiment is causing concern as is the increasing electoral successes of the far right Deutsches Volksunion and Republikaner parties. Their successes may simply be attributable to the disorientation caused by the unification process, especially in the east. Germany faces a plethora of elections in 1994 and it is only after that date that the true strength of the German far right will become clear. Meanwhile ugly scenes continue in German towns and cities, especially around the hostels for foreigners.

The National Front in France may simply be a vehicle for its leader Jean Marie Le Pen, but it too has seen its electoral support swell, especially in the southern French cities. Le Pen draws his support from the anti-immigrant vote and from those disenchanted with established politicians. Significantly, he became a leading figure in the campaign against the Maastricht treaty in advance of the French Referendum in September 1992.

Elsewhere in Europe nationalist sentiment is on the increase, partly in reaction to immigration from the south and east. Race riots scarred Brussels in 1991.

Centrifugal forces

Thus far the nationalisms discussed in western Europe have not been centrifugal phenomena. They are rather nationalisms that seek to exclude the social groups which do not correspond to the dominant type. However, centrifugal forces do exist in the states of western Europe. In the UK, for example, these are represented by Welsh, Scottish and more saliently Irish nationalism; in Spain by Basque and Catalan nationalist movements. At times these forces have appeared as acute problems, most notably through Irish Republican and Basque terrorism.

Belgium is a state riven by ethnic disputes between Flemish and French speaking populations. Tension between the two communities has made construction and survival of governments in Belgium difficult. The Belgian state has held together, partly through a fear of the alternative and partly through a devolution of power from the centre to the local communities. Academics have used the term 'consociationalism'[8] to describe the workings of democracies which seem to be unusually divided. It is a concept which may have relevance to the discussion of the state within the EC.

The state and the European Community

The supranational institutions of the EC have always caused attention to the dangers that the nation-state was losing its defining characteristic, namely its sovereignty.

Concerns over supranationalism, amongst other things, led Britain to delay its application to join the Community. The UK finally became a member in 1973. It has remained staunch in its adherence that the Community should be run on intergovernmental lines – that is the voluntary cooperation of sovereign states. While less vocal, other states have followed similar positions. In the 1960s De Gaulle provoked a crisis in the Community by protesting at the increasing powers of the Commission. The formula, known as the Luxembourg Compromise, which brought France back into the institutions of the Community, ensured that the intergovernmental Council of Ministers would continue to be the ultimate decision-making body and that states would have the power of veto on issues of singular national importance to them. The Committee of Permanent Representatives (COREPER) and the European Council reinforced this intergovernmentalism. The Commission retained important powers of initiative, thus leaving a supranational body a large degree of discretion over the agenda of the Community.

The intergovernmental nature of the Community frustrates those who wish to see a more federal Europe. There is a continuous tension between the adherents of both positions. What is clear is that membership of the Community does entail a loss of sovereignty through the absorption of Community law into national legislation. In addition, the scope of the Community's activities has progressively enlarged from its original, and still central, agricultural background. The European monetary system requires governments to maintain a stable currency, thus affecting the freedom of governments to set interest rates to promote recovery or to put pressure on borrowing. The 'single market' will eliminate the power of governments to covertly protect domestic industries through bureaucratic and costly customs procedures. Goods, services and people should be able to flow across borders within the Community without hindrance. The Community also now affects member states' freedom to set indirect taxation by establishing a minimum rate of value added tax (VAT) (although this system is not yet universal). The Maastricht Treaty, if implemented, will see the goals of the EC further cover many of the areas that traditionally are the preserve of nation-states: health, education, the environment, transport, industrial policy, consumer protection, for example.

The reactions against the growing integration of the Community, which accelerated after the events of 1989, have fallen into a sterile debate between those that claim a federal European super-state is in the making and those who agree but consider this the ultimate nightmare.[9] In fact, those that oppose Maastricht should look closely at the text which embodies the principle of 'subsidiarity':

> In areas which do not fall within its exclusive competence, the Community shall take action . . . only if and so far as the objectives of the proposed action cannot be sufficiently achieved by the member states and can therefore, by reason of the scale or effects of the proposed action, be better achieved by the Community.
>
> (*The Economist*, 11.7.92)

In part the debate over the European Community confuses sovereignty with national identity. It is ironic that the states of eastern and central Europe should be willing to join the EC after so recently and heroically recovering their national identities. Indeed, the growing list of potential members, which includes most of the states of central and eastern Europe, the EFTA countries and Cyprus, Malta and Turkey would suggest a terminal crisis of confidence in the European nation-state!

Other points need exploration. Existing member states such as Spain, Ireland, Portugal and Germany are using their membership of the Community to develop their own identity as separate states. If membership really means the surrender of sovereignty and national identity to a centralised and unaccountable body in Brussels, why are states so keen to do it? One answer is that states recognise that membership offers economic benefits within the internal market which could not otherwise be gained. Structural and regional funding also hold attractions to states.

Another answer might be that in reality the dichotomy that has been set up whereby any advances for the European Community inevitably weaken the authority of the nation-state is a false one. Taylor has argued persuasively that at the European level, state and international organisation are capable of being mutually reinforcing (Taylor 1991: 109). He contrasts two theories of integration – federalism and consociationalism – arguing that the latter is a more realistic explanation of the fate of the state in the EC (see the discussion of the federalist/confederalist approach in Chapter 6).

Both functionalism and federalism suggest a linear view of integration which proceeds progressively, either because of the increasing recognition of its functional value to members, or because of the adherence within an agreed set of rules or constitution which incrementally manages diversity with greater success.

Consociationalism, by contrast, explains the management of highly diverse groups but without predicting a linear progression to integration. The constituency and power base of the political elites is drawn from the various national components and thus relies on the continued protection of their autonomy. While the elites have an interest in ensuring that the Community is increasingly economically successful, this is largely to increase the returns for their sector. Thus an essentially political relationship is established between the representative elite and their constituents, and between the various representative elites. The progress of these relationships may be anything but linear. In the final analysis the various components hang together through fear of the consequences of break-up, particularly in view of their likely marginalisation from subsequent developments, and through recognition of the benefits of membership.

With respect to minorities, whether they be economic (trade unions) or national, the Community represents an arena of potential direct access where they can assert their identity and possibly increase the returns to their groups, although all this will be resisted by existing elites. The following quotation is illuminating with respect to the position of national minorities in the EC:

> Moves towards European Union are transforming ideas about what it means to be an independent state. A decade ago the Basque Nationalists would not have hesitated in saying their aim was outright independence. Today they prefer to be vague. They cannot just drop the dream of independence, for fear of losing support to the extremists. Europe allows

them to sidestep the issue . . . In 20–30 years, predicts Xabier Arzallus, the leader of the Basque Nationalist Party, there will not only be a European currency, but a European foreign policy and army. 'Why should we found a new state in the new Europe? The states will wither away.' Resisting the danger of economic marginalisation is a bigger challenge for the Basques, he reckons, than gaining independent statehood. In the corner of his office stands a European flag with 13 yellow stars instead of 12, a symbol of the Basques' desire to have a distinctive place in the European constellation.

(*The Economist* 1992a)

CONCLUSION

In conclusion, it is clear that the state survives in western Europe, even if the voluntary transfer of sovereignty to make domestic law does not fit established notions of the anatomy of statehood (Northedge 1976: 134). Consociationalism provides an explanation which emphasises the continued relevance of the state in the articulation, defence and satisfaction of national interests but through the process of negotiation within an institutional structure rather than in isolation.

The state per se certainly survives in eastern and central Europe, but individual states will continue to face threats to their existence. The eastern and central European states have not yet seen the benefits or have had the opportunities of anything greater than *ad hoc* international collaboration.

Notions of a pan-European future nevertheless have to take account of the enormous disparity between European states in wealth, stability, development, political arrangement and military power. Indeed some of the new states or the states that might yet be created in the east are so lacking in many of these attributes that their viability as separate states is in question.

NOTES

1   For a fuller discussion of the bloc discipline which affected members of both alliances during the Cold War see DePorte, A. (1979) *Europe Between the Superpowers*, or Halliday, F. (1986) *The Making of the Second Cold War*.

2   Canada and the USA are also members of the CSCE. Japan attended the July 1992 Conference as an honorary observer.

3   See Thatcher speech at College of Bruges, 30 September 1988, or Sked, A. (1990) *A Proposal for European Union, The Bruges Group, Occasional Paper 9*, or Taylor, P. (1991) 'The European Community and the state', *Review of International Studies*, 17, 2, April, 109–27.

4   *The Economist* (1992) 'Why the Danes wouldn't', 6 June, p.42.
5   For good surveys of the development of the European Community see Urwin, D. (1991) *The Community of Europe* and Nugent, N. (1991) *The Government and Politics of the European Community*.
6   Halliday, F. (1986) *The Making of the Second Cold War*.
7   There is a considerable literature on power in International Relations. See for example Wight, M. (1979) *Power Politics*, or Northedge, F. (1976) *The International Political System*, or Morgenthau, H. (1972) *Politics Among Nations*.
8   See Smith, G. (1990) *Politics in Western Europe* and Lijphart, A. (1969) 'Consociational Democracy', *World Politics*, 21, 207–25
9   Sked, A. (1990) '*A proposal for European union*', The Bruges Group, Occasional Paper, 9.

Chapter 4

The individual level

Individualism in European relations

David Armstrong and Stuart Croft

INTRODUCTION

The Cold War was seen on both sides as involving not simply a contest of military power but a struggle between two opposing sets of political, social and economic doctrines. In this sense the collapse of communism was widely perceived to entail a victory, not just of western might but of the western conception of right, which may be generally defined as the free pursuit by the individual of his/her own route to happiness within a liberal democratic framework which guaranteed his/her political and civil rights, and permitted the greatest material good for the greatest number to be attained through the workings of a market economy. Some even believed that the defeat of communism amounted, in a sense, to the final victory of the west, to the 'end of history', with no significant barriers remaining to the universal triumph of these ideas (see, for example, Fukuyama 1989). In particular, the enthusiastic embracing by eastern Europe of the classical western doctrines seemed to ensure that, for the first time, those ideals would prevail throughout the whole of the continent that gave birth to them.

If this were indeed the case, it would mean that a conclusion had at last been reached to the debate that has dominated European political and intellectual history since the Renaissance: the debate between a set of ideas that gave centre stage to the rights, needs and interests of the individual and the successive alternatives to this that have appeared over the centuries. This chapter will seek to outline the general development of these ideas to set out the dimensions of what may be taken as a west European ideal with regard to individualism. However, it will then be suggested that such an ideal is deeply contested within western Europe; although this ideal of individualism it is suggested in the third section is widely seen as a model to the new regimes in eastern Europe and the former Soviet Union. Inevitably, then, the arguments over the individual versus the collective will continue in the post-Cold War period despite the collapse of communism and the 'triumph' of western ideas.

THE HISTORICAL DEVELOPMENT OF INDIVIDUALISM

Individualism, as it emerged in the seventeenth century and developed during the following two centuries, was both a set of theories and a political and economic programme. These two aspects, however, were never kept entirely separate, since the theorists were invariably influenced by contemporary events, while individualist ideas constantly intruded into the language and policies of governments and their opponents. This was as true in the 1980s as it had been in the 1780s, when the American Constitution was framed, or in the 1680s, when Locke wrote 'The Two Treatises of Government'. It is therefore necessary to pay some attention to both the theoretical bases of individualism and its various practical ramifications.

In the seventeenth century, individualism was primarily a doctrine with religious, political and moral facets. At the end of the eighteenth century, it began to acquire an important economic dimension, and the nineteenth century saw additional notions, such as German 'romantic individuality', appear. Without attempting even a brief history of these developments, it is possible to distinguish five disparate components of the approach that are relevant in this context (see in part the discussion in Lukes 1973: 45–114).

The first is the central moral principle that underlies individualism, namely that there is no higher value than individual worth. Many of the great *cause célèbre* of European political history have at root concerned the individual's fight for justice (for example, Dreyfus and Solzhenitsyn). In the definitive formulation of this idea by Kant:

> man, and in general every rational being, exists as an end in himself, not merely as a means for arbitrary use by this or that will: he must in all his actions whether they are directed to himself or to other rational beings, always be viewed at the same time as an end. Persons, therefore, are not merely subjective ends whose existence as an effect of our actions has a value for us: they are objective ends – that is things whose existence is in itself an end.

(quoted in Lukes 1973: 49)

Second in importance is political individualism. This has had many consequences for western political theory and practice but amongst the most significant are the idea that legitimate government only exists by virtue of the consent of the governed, the related notion of a social contract, the principles that government should be representative and democratic, and that individuals possess certain rights and interests which it is the sole purpose of government to advance and protect. These were the ideas, first enunciated systematically by Locke, that underpinned the American Declaration of Independence and the French Revolution's Declaration of the Rights of Man and of Citizens.

These ideas were no less powerful some two hundred years later, when they helped to determine western strategy in offering the poisoned chalice known as Basket Three of the Helsinki Final Act to the Soviets. The Soviets believed that they had obtained from Helsinki international legitimacy for communist control over eastern Europe in return for agreeing to participate in conventional arms control and acceptance of a seemingly innocuous human rights 'basket'. In effect, however, the Helsinki process gave the west a legitimate right to concern itself with human rights in eastern Europe and formally integrated human rights issues into general east–west relations. Although the treatment of individuals in the eastern bloc after 1975 varied – with many a major *cause célèbre* such as Sakharov and Havel – when the thaw in the east began, many east European governments responded to western pressure during the 1986–9 Vienna Conference on Security and Cooperation in Europe (CSCE) meeting over human rights by freeing political prisoners, increasing emigration, ending radio jamming and increasing toleration of religious activities. Further, it was in support of the human rights basket that groups within the Soviet Union and eastern Europe organised in defiance of national governments, beginning or perhaps accelerating a process of opposition to communist rule that reached its climax between 1989 and 1991.[1]

Economic individualism, the third main tenet of the individualist approach to political life, has both normative and theoretical aspects. It asserts that economies should be based upon the pursuit by individuals of their own self-interest since that is the only way in which the genuine preferences of people (as opposed to those that legislators believe they have or should have) can make themselves felt. It also advances the hypothesis that market forces, the sole ordering device permitted in an individualistic economic system, will produce a more efficient allocation of resources through the working of the price mechanism than is possible in any planned economy, other than one managed by an all-knowing and all-powerful deity. In the classic statement by Adam Smith (which is also more generally applicable to individualism):

The man of system . . . seems to imagine that he can arrange the different members of a great society with as much ease as the hand arranges the different pieces upon a chessboard. He does not consider that the pieces upon the chessboard have no other principle of motion besides that which the hand impresses upon them; but that, in the great chessboard of human society, every single piece has a principle of motion of its own, altogether different from that which the legislature might choose to impress upon it. If these two principles coincide and act in the same direction, the game of human society will go on easily and harmoniously, and is very likely to be happy and successful. If they are opposite or different, the game will go on miserably and the society must be at all times in the highest degree of disorder.

(cited in Hayek 1973: 35)

The fourth and most modern component of individualism is privacy, defined by Lukes as 'an area within which the individual is or should be left alone by others and able to do and think whatever he chooses' (Lukes 1973: 59). Of course defining the nature of that area has been a task of great complexity, confused further by the technological ability of machinery to store vast amounts of information on the lives and abilities of individuals. Further, individual privacy is often violated by the popular press which in western Europe, unlike its former Soviet bloc counterparts, has tended to focus on stories relating to individuals rather than collectives; on, for example, a particular individual's sexual propriety rather than the achievement of an economic production target by a particular collective. Whereas there are laws in some western European countries to protect individual privacy against media intrusion (in Denmark, France since 1970, while in Germany individuals have had a right of reply dating back to the nineteenth century), this is by no means generalised in Europe and is by no means always a guarantee of privacy.

Finally, reference should be made to the set of theoretical propositions known as 'methodological individualism'. These 'claim that all social phenomena – whether process, structure, institution or habitus – can be explained by the actions and properties of the participating individuals' (Elster 1990: 47). Methodological individualism, therefore, purports to be an explanatory hypothesis and so should be of interest mainly to theorists. However, in certain respects it can be as subversive as the other components of individualism since, by rejecting explanations of phenomena that rely upon a social or collective interpretation, it undermines the entire theoretical basis of all collectivist approaches to society. Given that its high priests include Schumpeter, Hayek and Popper, this outcome is not, perhaps, surprising. When the former British Prime Minister, Margaret Thatcher, made her famous utterance to the effect that there was 'no such thing as society', she was, consciously or not, revealing herself to be a methodological individualist.

Individualist ideas first emerged in Europe as counters to the arbitrary power of kings and the claims of the church to a higher wisdom than any one person could aspire to. Such ideas have never lacked opponents since then, although the force of their central proposition – that any exercise of political authority must ultimately be capable of being justified by reference to the rights and interests of individuals – has been such that even some of individualism's leading enemies have felt it necessary to pay lipservice to the doctrine. Mussolini, for example, tried to argue that, although fascism opposed 'all the individualistic abstractions of a materialistic nature, like those of the eighteenth century', it was not against the individual as such. Full realisation of individuality came through embracing the 'spiritual process' of history, which meant, essentially, complete identification with the state:

> Against Individualism, the Fascist conception is for the State. It is opposed to classical Liberalism, which arose from the necessity of reacting against absolutism, and which brought its historical purpose to an end when the State was transformed into the conscience and will of the people. Liberalism denied the State in the interests of the particular individual; Fascism reaffirms the State as the true reality of the individual.
>
> (Quoted in Oakeshott 1939: 166)

Other criticisms of individualism have come from many quarters, only a few of which may be briefly summarised here. Conservative objections, such as those advanced by Burke and other opponents of the French Revolution, tended to focus upon the dangers of unfettered personal freedom for the orderly society. Social reformers in the nineteenth century believed that individuals left to themselves in the more arduous and complex conditions of that time would never be able to obtain such benefits as decent housing, health care, fair working conditions and protection for women and children. Socialists thought that the right to property, which had been seen by Locke as a right equal to the other principal human rights, was no longer as valid in an era of enormous capital accumulation as it had been when property meant, essentially, small holdings of land. Marx believed that emphasising individual rights would only serve to separate the individual from his/her social, and, in particular, his/her class identity. Even more strongly than other nineteenth-century socialists, he also saw economic individualism as, in practice, leading inevitably to great wealth for the few at the expense of misery and poverty for the many. Religious and other moral criticisms of individualism came from those who saw the doctrine as emphasising only means while ignoring ends, such as God's purpose for humanity or the 'good society'. This was not, incidentally, a problem for Hayek, who argued:

> It is often made a reproach to the Great Society and its market order that it lacks an agreed ranking of ends. This, however, is in fact its great merit which makes individual freedom and all it values possible. The Great Society arose through the discovery that men can live together in peace and mutually benefiting each other without agreeing on the particular aims which they severally pursue.
>
> (Hayek 1976: 109)

In the twentieth century, opponents of individualism ranged from National Socialists, who saw the individual's true identity as subsumed by membership of his/her race, and denied the principle that all individuals were of equal worth, to pragmatists, who thought that separating an individual from society was logically fallacious since the vast range of human needs and wants in the modern era could only be satisfied through their provision by society as a whole. However, in the second half of the twentieth century, the most profound and sustained confrontation has been between the western conceptions – based on individualism – of human rights, liberal democracy and the market economy, and the alternatives offered by the communist societies of the Soviet Union and eastern Europe.

Like many other opponents of western doctrines, the Soviet bloc did not deny the validity of human rights, democracy and the other corollaries of individualism; rather they claimed that their genuine and complete attainment was only possible within a communist system. This assertion was not seen at first as so far-fetched as it now appears, and many continued to believe that progress in certain areas was being made in the communist states, even after the revelations about the extent of Stalin's genocide, the suppression of the Hungarian uprising, the building of the Berlin Wall and the crushing of the Prague Spring. The essential Soviet bloc claims were, first, that the reality in the west did not live up to the ideology – democracy was 'bourgeois' and served the interests of capitalists, rights were denied to numerous groups, equality was meaningless where there were huge disparities of wealth. Secondly (following Marx), the individual was alienated from society in the west and would only be able to realise his/her full potential within a collective, socialist framework. Thirdly, the Soviet Union and its partners guaranteed numerous economic and social rights, such as the rights to work, to housing, to leisure and to education, which were barely recognised as rights in the west. The classic western civil and political rights were also acknowledged in successive Soviet constitutions, but with severe qualifications. The 1977 Constitution, for example, declared that such rights must be exercised 'in accordance with the interests of the people – to strengthen and develop the socialist system', that they 'must not harm the interests of society and the State', and that they did not include the right to engage in 'anti-Soviet agitation and propaganda' or to repeat 'deliberate fabrications which discredit the Soviet political and social system' (cited in Rees 1986: 64).

The Cold War was thus, in part, characterised by a debate between two opposing conceptions of the relationship between the individual and society, and of the nature of human rights. Gorbachev, Shevardnadze and other Soviet leaders in the period from 1988 to 1991 came close to openly acknowledging that, in this contest, it was the western standpoint that had prevailed and this was certainly the general assumption in both east and west after the collapse of the Soviet Union in 1991. Given the prominence of the debate over human rights in the last two decades of the Cold War, this meant that rights would inevitably be an important consideration in the new European situation. The apparent 'victory' of political and civil rights over economic and social rights also implied that the former would be seen as more significant in the process of reconstruction in the east. Finally, as such rights were supposedly already firmly in place in the liberal democracies of western Europe, it could be comfortably assumed that those societies provided a ready-made working model which could be simply adopted wholesale by eastern Europe.

It is open to serious doubt whether such easy assumptions about the triumph of individualist values are valid, even in the western European context, still less in eastern Europe. It may even be that one outcome of the end of the Cold War has been for attention to shift to problematical aspects of the individualist 'model' in western Europe, and for questions to arise about its applicability or even desirability in eastern Europe. The long debate over the individualist thesis, in other words, is far from ended.

THE WEST EUROPEAN DEBATE OVER INDIVIDUALISM

In the western European ideal, the rights of the individual are protected primarily by the principle of the rule of law. This insures the individual against arbitrary and inhumane treatment and guarantees equality before the law. If there is some flaw in the legal redress available to the individual in his/her own country, west Europeans are uniquely entitled to take their case to an international court, the European Court of Human Rights, whose decisions have caused many European states to improve still further the legal protection enjoyed by their citizens. Such was the importance of law in western polities that in his reform process Gorbachev made it central, calling for the Soviet Union to become a 'rule of law state' and extending the concept by declaring in the UN that 'our ideal is a world community of States which are based on the rule of law' (Gorbachev 1988: 7).

However, even in this most fundamental context there is at least one area in which the ideal is heavily compromised by the practice: the struggle against terrorism. In Britain, for example, suspected Irish Republican Army (IRA) terrorists receive less than the complete range of legal rights available to people accused of other crimes. The 'legal' spokesmen and women of Irish Republicanism are also denied by law access to the mass media. Other tactics have been employed against the IRA which would not find a place in any handbook of the perfect liberal state (see Kearns 1991). While it is certainly true that the majority in Britain accept that such compromises are required in order to fight the greater evil, an important concession has, none the less, been made in accepting that there are circumstances short of all-out war in which the rights of the individual may be suspended. Disquiet about the consequences of such steps has increased in Britain with successive revelations about the wrongful imprisonment of numerous suspected terrorists: Julie Ward, the Guildford Four, the Birmingham Six and the MacGuire Seven. But Britain is not alone in this. Criticisms of the treatment of individuals suspected of terrorism over the period since the Helsinki process began have been heard in West Germany, Italy, Spain and France. Thus it may be suggested that in some circumstances the rights of the individual may be dependent upon the nature of the action or crime of which the individual is accused.

Even if it may be argued that this is the exception that proves the rule, there are numerous other respects in which individualist doctrines remain problematical in western Europe. For example, one of the fiercest and most difficult debates over human rights since the Second World War has been between those who adhere to the traditional view which stresses purely individual rights and those who claim that, if an individual suffers injustice by virtue of his/her membership of a group, then the group as such should be accorded rights and the means to obtain justice as a group. The rationale for this view is:

> that the language and theory of the protection of human rights de-
> veloped in a time and place (England in the seventeenth century) when
> the issue was seen as one of deprivation because of conscience, because
> of individual decision and action, rather than one of deprivation because
> of race, colour or national origin. England was relatively homogenous

except for religion and political attitudes which largely flowed from religious conviction. These were seen as individual decisions, and to protect diversity was seen as an issue of protecting the diversity that flowed from individual decisions.

(Glazer 1978: 90)

Hence, it is argued, in societies where individuals cannot realise their full rights because of prejudice against the group to which they belong, the group itself should be protected. Where this principle begins to cause problems for individualism is when it is asserted that particular groups should actually be privileged in some sense because that is the only way in which individual members of the group may achieve justice. For example, pressure to introduce equal opportunities legislation that seeks to ensure that the members of a disadvantaged group are given employment in preference to other groups because of past discrimination, as in the United States, could be said to introduce a new form of discrimination: against those non-group members failing to secure employment even with equal or superior qualifications.

A related issue concerns the desire of many ethnic groups to see their identity as a group recognised and protected through, for example, the provision of special schools and acknowledgement of their distinct values and cultures in existing educational programmes and other forums. Traditional individualism is colour blind and ignores ethnic differences; its ideal society is an integrated one in which people retain their individuality but have equal rights before the law. The concept of multiculturalism argues, in effect, that this ideal cannot, and perhaps should not, be attained in a multi-ethnic community since individual dignity is partly dependent upon recognition of the dignity of the group. Without such recognition, the rights of the individual might depend upon the ethnicity of the individual.

Another kind of group identity which has been strongly argued is based on gender rather than race. Feminist arguments are many and varied but, to the extent that they have a common core, it is the claim that mere legal equality is not sufficient to safeguard women's rights and that women have needs distinct from those of men and these needs, too, require recognition. One aspect of this debate that encapsulates the issues in the context of this chapter concerns sexual violence against women. Some feminists would argue, first, that this is uniquely a problem for women: many cities in western Europe have virtually no-go areas for women alone at night, which makes a mockery of the individual's right to travel freely. Secondly, when a case relating to sexual violence goes to trial, the victims frequently feel that they are forced to defend their own lifestyles and behaviour against the defence lawyers. On the other hand, the legal rights of the accused are absolutely fundamental in western jurisprudence and, it might be argued, if lawyers were unable to ask searching questions of victims, the rights of the man on trial might suffer. It may also be the case that, in a legal system which favoured women victims rather than the defendants, the unscrupulous might be able to use false charges against men for their own purposes. Such emotive charges and counter-charges are already common in the United States (in 1991–2 for example, in the cases of William Kennedy Smith, Mike Tyson and Judge Clarence Thomas which all attracted great publicity). The danger to which feminists might point is that a focus on individualism ignores the reality that in a variety of situations the rights of the individual will depend upon the gender of that individual.

Perhaps even more so than arguments over ethnic identity, the debate over the validity of gender as a means of group identification are contested in western Europe. Nevertheless, it is notable that those women's movements that have emerged in eastern Europe either on a city basis (in Moscow and St. Petersburg, for example) or, more slowly, on a national basis (as in Poland), do not look to traditional western ideas about political and civil rights of individuals but rather to the tactics and strategies of their sister organisations in western Europe.

The Roman Catholic Church, which was one of several bastions of established authority against which individual rights were first asserted in the fifteenth and sixteenth centuries, has remained an important factor in the debate over rights to the present day. On the one hand, it supported oppressed individuals and movements to replace communism with western style individualism, as in Poland and elsewhere in the former Soviet bloc. On the other hand, it has taken stands against certain kinds of assertions of individual rights. It will not accept the ordination of women; it opposes a woman's right to choose over abortion; and it is hostile to the rights of individuals to divorce. A case that brought the most fiercely argued of these issues, abortion, to the fore occurred in Ireland in 1992. Ireland's constitutional ban on abortion led the family of a teenage rape victim to attempt to organise an abortion in England. Such efforts were met with legal attempts to prevent the girl's freedom of movement on the grounds that it was her purpose to arrange an abortion; this was despite the Single European Act and the principle of free movement of people between states within the European Community. At issue in this case were two kinds of confrontation. The first was between the rights of the individual and the rights of the collective (the Catholic state of Ireland). The second was between the rights of one individual, the girl, and those of what in some eyes was another individual, the unborn child.

Yet another contentious area in western Europe concerns the right to privacy. This is challenged primarily by the communications revolution which has given numerous public and private organizations the power to subject individuals to various novel forms of harassment and intrusion. The potential benefits to humanity from these technological developments are immense yet they also raise in a new form an ancient dilemma of individualism: if a collective good of perhaps great importance can be attained by denying to individuals the full and complete realisation of an acknowledged right, should this count as a net gain to society or a net loss to the individual? How is the balance between the two to be measured?

This, of course, is, in essence, the same question as that still posed by European Social Democratic and non-communist socialist parties, which, if they stand for anything, must uphold the view that some goods can only be provided on a collective basis if all in society are to enjoy them. This therefore requires an important role for the state. Hayek, perhaps the most influential of the individualist philosophers, reserves some of his greatest scorn for the view that 'society' is more capable than market forces of determining a just distribution of goods and services:

> I believe that 'social justice' will ultimately be recognized as a will-o'-the-wisp which has lured men to abandon many of the values which in the past have inspired the development of civilization . . . like most attempts to pursue an unattainable goal, the striving for it will also produce highly undesirable consequences, and in particular lead to the destruction of the indispensable environment in which the traditional moral values alone can flourish, namely personal freedom.
>
> (Hayek 1976: 67)

While few pragmatic politicians would go quite so far with Hayek along the individualist road, there can be little doubt that collectivism has staged a significant retreat in Europe in recent years. Not only has communism collapsed in the east; socialist parties in the west have been subjected to a series of electoral setbacks, with the only successes coming when collectivism has been all but abandoned (Mitterrand in France, Gonzalez in Spain: see Schmidt 1990 and Gillespie 1990). Yet socialist parties remain as significant opposition groups and, while few would now argue for wholesale nationalisation of industry, the essential issues that have been raised by socialist thinkers cannot be dismissed quite so easily in the real world of hard choices, imperfection and compromise as they can by taking the individualist philosophy to its logical conclusion. Of what use is freedom of movement to a disabled person if central provision is not made to facilitate movement? Of what use is freedom of the press to someone who cannot read because of inadequate state provision of education? Is the freedom of an impoverished, black, single mother really identical to that of the son of a white millionaire? Can a spontaneous market order provide adequate protection from environmental pollution?

It should also be noted that there remains one important bastion of collectivism in western Europe: the European Community, whose Commission has adopted an increasingly interventionist stance and which agreed at the Maastricht summit in December 1991 (with the exception of Britain) social legislation with far-reaching provisions for the protection of groups in employment. Yet even here collectivism is under attack, with 'subsidiarity' the weapon. Reducing decision making to the lowest level of government possible increases the power of individuals, it is suggested. Whether this is true – or whether subsidiarity is merely meant to concentrate power in the hands of national governments rather than the European Commission – it is nevertheless the case that individualism remains an important part of the language of political debate in western Europe (see, in part, Pond 1992 and Tiersky 1992).

A final problematical aspect of individual rights in western Europe concerns the position of migrants and would-be migrants. Immigration has been an issue that has cyclically reached high political prominence in western Europe, and in the 1990s tensions are again high particularly in France and to a lesser extent Germany. The key question that all states have had to face is this: how does an individual from outside western Europe become a citizen of western Europe, and therefore share in all the rights and privileges associated with such citizenship? How should criteria be set up for immigration: on grounds of wealth, skills, family ties with those already in western Europe? Should new immigrants be assimilated into the predominant culture, or be allowed to create subcultures which may support views in opposition to those in society at large? Much of this debate has focused on Islam within western Europe, although in reality it has tended to focus upon more radical sections within the Muslim community. However, whether the collective Islamic community should have the right to prohibit the publication of a book by Salman Rushdie that is either blasphemous to the collective, or the art of the individual, has been and is a live issue that may only be one of a series of such confrontations within western Europe.[2]

Although in the past much of the immigration issue has been focused upon the relationship of western Europe with various groups and countries in the South, in the future the immigration issue is likely to be bound up at least as much with the relationship with post-communist Europe. For forty years the idea of free movement of peoples has been central to western

Europes' attempts to obtain the moral high ground over the east with regard to human rights. Now, in the post-Cold War period, the arguments are slightly different. Whereas east–west movement of peoples was once precluded by the actions of the east, with the exception of further westward migration of ethnic Germans, it will now be precluded by the actions of the west. All in western Europe fear the mass migration of peoples. The rights of individuals to move becomes something of a threat if multiplied by several million. During the 1970s and early 1980s, only about 100,000 people left the countries of the Warsaw Pact each year. In 1989 this leapt to 1.2 million (Widgren 1990: 757). Instability and conflict in the countries of the former Warsaw Pact could lead to a further increase, along the line seen in 1992 as refugees have left Croatia and particularly Bosnia–Hercegovina (by mid-1992 over a quarter of a million had fled to Germany alone). Whereas the focus is usually on the destabilising effects this might have on the societies of western Europe, it should be recognised that for many in the former Soviet Union, or in other countries such as Romania, an attractive option is to move to countries such as Poland and the Czech and Slovak Federal Republic (CSFR), with all the possible negative connotations for those countries. Estimates of emigration from the former Soviet Union range from 1.5 million to 7 million (Larrabee 1992: 7). How this is managed will say a great deal about the role of the individual in the new Europe, and indeed the relationship between post-communist Europe and its more prosperous neighbours.

There is therefore a great deal of dispute over the nature of rights within western Europe. Agreement can perhaps be seen much more in negative rather than positive terms. Political influence over the legal process and conviction without trial, the absence of a recognisable democratic system and the freedom of the press, inequality before the law and the show trial, torture and summary execution, all these are guaranteed to be defined in western Europe as infringements of the rights of the individual. However, dispute arises when other groups within western Europe profess support for more collectivist approaches to the question of rights. In other words, that which is seen to be defined as a right in western Europe depends upon the perspective taken. For some, individual rights are supreme; but for many other groups, they have to be seen in the context of collective rights. The categorisation of the Cold War period – the west supporting the idea of individual and political rights, the east collective economic and social rights – is therefore an inadequate way to understand the nature of the debate over the rights of individuals *vis-à-vis* their state in western Europe. But many in western Europe would support their notion of the relationship between the individual and the state being exported to eastern Europe whether it be in terms of greater freedom of markets, or support for humanitarian intervention in civil disorder such as that in the former Yugoslavia. All of this much complicates the debate over the place of the individual in eastern Europe.

INDIVIDUALISM IN EASTERN EUROPE

Since the collapse of communism in eastern Europe in 1989 and the collapse of the Soviet Union itself in 1991, new leaderships have come to power in the successor regimes and states with a variety of difficult economic and political tasks. They have, almost without exception, sought to fashion what the east central Europeans have called a 'return to Europe', by which it has been meant a reintegration of the continent in political, economic and social terms (see Hyde-Price 1991). A part of this has related to the redefinition of the rights of individuals in relation to the states; however, this has had by definition to be part of a broader approach to the restructuring of nations. One problem has been the relationship between declining economic bases, as economies have been privatised and liberalised, and political interpretations of this, in the context of societies where underemployment was the norm, but unemployment almost unheard of. The tensions that have resulted have been complicated by the involvement of western ideas and activists. A second problem has been political, as leaders have wrestled with the challenge of defining how much democracy was appropriate to their societies and the stability of their regimes. Yet a third problem has related to nationalities, as nations and states rarely coincide in eastern Europe.

As radical economic transformation has been introduced in eastern Europe it has brought with it widespread disillusionment as unemployment has risen, as wages have fallen, and as the problems of feeding families have rarely been solved. Partly this was predictable, particularly in those nations that have decided to move to an almost immediate transformation without much cushioning, such as Poland. Many of those from the west who have acted in advisory capacities to the new governments have identified the money supply and privatisation as essentially the greatest problems, needing to be dealt with before any growth could be achieved. Undoubtedly this has begun building up pressure and resentment, as those elements of life that were traditionally accepted as being part of the rights of members of those societies no longer exist. In other words a change of culture is being created by economic hardship, exacerbated by previous experience, a phenomenon most particularly felt by those countries experiencing the fastest transformation as individuals are forced to readjust their views of the nature of their economic rights. This exacerbation of problems by imposing western European norms on eastern European circumstances relates not only to economic issues. A freer press has led to an explosion of pornography in countries such as Hungary, and a more general growth of that which in western Europe is generally referred to as the 'gutter press'. Supporters of the 'Pro-Life' movement have entered the tense debates over abortion rights in countries such as Poland. The Roman Catholic Church has sought to re-establish norms and values that were illegitimate and not emphasised in the underground Church during communist rule. For example, in the CSFR many priests and bishops who kept the Church alive through underground activity during the communist period have, since late 1991, been purged from the Church. Partly in order to disguise the members of the underground Church, many priests married. Since married priests are in general unacceptable to Rome, many priests – including the outspoken Bishop Zahradnik, who spent six years in jail for his beliefs under the communists – have been removed from office despite, in some parts of Bohemia, over 60 per cent of parishes unable to find any priest. Individuals who were acceptable during the difficult times have quickly been discarded in the cause of conformity.

The second issue has related to the question of implementing a democratic system and legislating for rights in the post-communist states. Broadly two strategies seem to have been followed: to democratise widely (Hungary, and the CSFR – see, for example, Simai 1992), or to democratise narrowly largely as a legitimising device (Romania and Bulgaria). Popular movements to agitate for more fundamental democratic transformation have often been dealt with through violence, whether it be through miners acting on the urging of the Romanian government in Bucharest in 1990, the militia firing in support of President Gamsakhurdia on protestors in Georgia in late 1991, or violence against Islamic protestors in Tajikistan in 1992. In much of the Balkans and the former Soviet Union, protesting against government policy is still not conducive to furthering personal safety. Similarly, legal reform has been pursued in a differentiated fashion, although all governments agree on the need to get away from the Soviet-style approach to the question of individual rights: 'Civil rights shall be protected by law except as they are exercised in contradiction to their purpose in socialist society in the period of communist construction' (from the 1961 law code *Fundamentals of Legislation of the USSR and the Union Republics*).

The final challenge has related to implementing a system of rights for populations where different loyalties are expressed. In much of eastern Europe many seem to share a political culture which emphasises loyalty to a particular group which may form only a portion of the state rather than to concepts applicable to all. In other words, there seems to be a lack of nation-building about many entities in eastern Europe. This has been borne out by the events since 1989: three states have disappeared (the German Democratic Republic, Yugoslavia and the Soviet Union) and centrifugal forces threaten many others, from the CSFR to the Russian Federation. In relation to these problems, a prescription emanating from western Europe for eastern Europe that focuses on the old Cold War agenda of individual rights seems out of place. This is, of course, not to argue that undemocratic authoritarian regimes with widespread abuses of human rights in eastern Europe would or should be a matter of indifference to those in western Europe; rather it suggests that the approach in western Europe is much more collective than is sometimes portrayed, and that emphasis on greater collectivism rather than classical individualism may be more in keeping with the culture and the problems of eastern Europe. As Geza Jeszensky, later Hungarian Foreign Minister, and others argued in their Christmas 1989 democratic manifesto:

> in Eastern Europe all swear by freedom of conscience, civil liberties, democracy, a free economy, the observance of human rights and self-determination . . . One of the cardinal pre-requisites of democracy is tolerance for those whose political beliefs, religion or language differs – for the various minorities. The practical realization of this principle is through the recognition of these groups' organization and autonomy in order to facilitate their free development.
>
> (Jeszensky 1992: 7–8)

In other words, particularly in the eastern European context where minority problems abound, democratisation and the role of the individual cannot be divided from the group context.

A particular danger is thus of moving rapidly to the individualist ethos at the expense of social cohesion in eastern Europe, partly as Burke argued with reference to France 200 years ago. Greater collectivism would lessen some of the shocks to the vulnerable polities that have been outlined above; greater individualism may only work imperfectly in societies where the self is often subsumed in a larger entity (the nation – which only rarely will encompass the entire state). It may well be that, as the problems of eastern Europe become more clear, policy-makers in western Europe will speak less about individual rights, the language of the Cold War, and more in terms of collective rights for national minorities in order to attempt to limit inter-ethnic strife, with all the attendant dangers of violence and destruction and, by extension, of migration to western Europe (see, in part, Snyder 1992).

CONCLUSION

The end of the Cold War has brought about little change to the concept of the individual within western Europe. As suggested above, there is a rich debate, one that is many centuries old, and this will undoubtedly continue. However, the collapse of communism has brought about important changes in the way in which the concept of the individual in western Europe may be seen as a solution to the problems of eastern Europe. The dialogue of the Cold War debate in western Europe was conducted in terms of the human rights of the individual in the east. Yet as suggested above, this may well be inappropriate in the post-communist era, with rights much more focused on groups in the east.

Much of this analysis has used the term 'eastern Europe'. Convenient as a label during the Cold War, it is now of relatively little utility except as a label which denotes 'not part of western Europe', in the sense that 'Third World' used to describe the world not primarily engaged in the central east–west division and competition during the Cold War. In describing and analysing a debate over the impact of individualism on the countries outside western Europe, a far finer series of distinctions are required. Some states – particularly the CSFR and Poland – have emerged from that which Havel called the 'post-totalitarian state' with leadership rooted in the anti-communist dissident movements. For such leaderships, legality and the individual are of importance. The dissident movements sought to 'defend anyone who is being prosecuted for acting in the spirit of rights . . . by insisting over and over again that the regime recognize and respect human and civil rights' (Havel 1990: 96; see also Michnik 1990). Yet even here there are problems, with the nationalist leadership in Slovakia illustrating less commitment to the liberalism of the dissident movements, while Poland struggles to develop stable government. In other states, where the communist elite largely reformulated itself – Romania, Ukraine, Serbia – the roots of the commitment to rights are much more shallow. It is in these countries where cynics might suggest that individualism is important as long as it allows populist leaders to maintain their power base; should that base be questioned, the reversion to authoritarianism and organised violence might be swift indeed. The victory of the values of the dissidents – and by extension the west – is therefore not widely evident, and may be short-lived even where they are strongest.

It is somewhat ironic, however, that the intelligentsia who led much of the opposition to communism have done much to legitimise individualism in its traditional form in the post-communist world. Ironic since nearly all were politically liberal or social democratic: yet the fall from short-lived power for many of the dissidents illustrates the power of the political right in many parts of the post-communist world to take the notions of individualism much further than the dissidents themselves would by and large have sought. In much of eastern Europe where dissidents have been influential, political debate by 1992 could often be characterised by dissident attempts to maintain some collectivist approaches to minimise the impact of individualism, particularly in its economic guise. This is as true for Russia as for Poland or the CSFR. Yet for the political right, only the full and speedy imposition of individualism will bring about a full transition to west European style states, and only such efforts would bring about the assistance in economic and political terms from the west that all agree is central to the economic development of the former communist part of Europe.

The political right in eastern Europe may have made an accurate political assessment at least in terms of the relationship of the post-communist states with the west. It would seem that the west, through the International Monetary Fund (IMF), the World Bank, the G7 (the seven leading industrial powers) as well as in bilateral relations, has shown its determination to promote 'good governance' in eastern Europe. By this it is meant that government is responsive to the rights and interests of individuals and encourages the development of a market economy. Yet by making economic assistance conditional upon eastern Europe developing liberal democracies and reforming their economies, such efforts have created two major dilemmas. The first is that the efforts of those on the political right in many countries of eastern Europe, encouraged by those in the west, will if a change of course does not occur create in some states a far more liberal and individualistic culture than exists in western Europe. The ideal of individualism in western Europe, contradictions and all, may then be imposed upon societies where the social fabric, after between forty-five and seventy-five years of communism, is already very weak. The 'monetarist' experiment of Pinochet in Chile, encouraged by experts from the west, which created massive unemployment and repression to create stability and growth, should stand as a model against imposing outside ideals on eastern Europe. The second problem is that the west's encouragement of 'good governance' is, in effect, a kind of international social engineering to help foster a form of government, and in particular a type of economy, whose basic principles hold in low regard the utility of such social engineering. This might be dismissed as a mere intellectual puzzle, were it not for the possibility that western intervention could eventually provoke unpredictable reactions in the east. As the venomous hatred that has been unleashed in the former Yugoslavia and in the Caucasus demonstrates, the reality in Europe is that powerful emotions linked to ethnic identities retain their capacity to dictate events, even in supposed 'models' of the western ideal, such as Spain or Britain.

Even without these kinds of paradoxes, tensions and problems inherent in individualism that have been identified here, a final difficulty might still remain. Implicit in individualist ideas is an assumption that most individuals, most of the time, will behave rationally: their choices will be determined essentially by self-interest. But if, in both parts of Europe, this is not the case – rationality for many being dependent upon group identification rather than any higher form of logic – much of the force of individualism is lost. Is there an essential rationality that is separate from a Serb or Croat rationality? Is the solution to political and economic decay and collapse in eastern Europe political democratisation and economic free markets based upon the elements of individualism set out in the first part of this chapter? Or is the problem much more ethnicity and nationality problems that have their own rationality, their own logic? Would the creation of a liberal democracy in Armenia and Azerbaijan prevent the bloody conflict that, in different forms, is many centuries old?

This is of course not to argue that democracy and the market economy hold no solutions to Europe's problems; but it is to question whether the expansion of individualism by itself is any real panacea to the dilemmas of eastern Europe. In any case, is it not a legitimate choice of an individual to subsume his or her identity into a large group?

Individualism remains a contentious issue in Europe, not just because of a conspiracy by bureaucrats, authoritarians and collectivists to deny people their rights but because individuals stubbornly cling to their identities as members of different kinds of groups. The fragmentation of Yugoslavia is clear evidence of this, but it is hardly likely to be the last occasion in Europe when blood is spilt not in defence of the rights of the individual but to enable individuals to belong to the particular national entity to which they have the strongest emotional bonds. Similarly, state provision of health care, education and social welfare exists, not because people are too ignorant to appreciate that absolute justice is a chimera but because most of them want there to be at least some safeguards against obvious deprivation. Such provision is as much a consequence of genuine choice as the outcome of market processes are claimed to be by leading proponents of individualism, such as Hayek. To move to the more extreme versions of individualism in eastern Europe would thus be highly destabilising for the societies involved. In the past the debate over individualism has often taken the form of a confrontation between the opposed but equally important imperatives of order and freedom. In Europe, in this sense at least, the debate continues.

NOTES

1   For example, the Soviet Helsinki Monitoring Group, the Polish KOR (Committee for Social Self-Defence) and, of course, Charter 77 in Czechoslovakia.
2   The book referred to is that by Salman Rushdie (1988) *The Satanic Verses*, London: Viking. See also James Piscatori (1990) 'The Rushdie affair and the politics of ambiguity', *International Affairs*, 66, 1, 767–89.

Part II

The issue agenda

Chapter 5

The military security agenda
Colin McInnes

INTRODUCTION

What is security? For the starving in Africa, security is food. For the homeless, security is shelter. For the stockmarket, security is stability and economic growth. Security is defined by the user, not just in terms of the amount of security required in order to be safe, but in terms of the very nature of security itself. For policy-makers and academic strategists in the west during the Cold War, the nature of security was unproblematic. Security was the absence of war with the Soviet Union. The key questions therefore concerned not the nature of security, but the amount of security required. But with the end of the Cold War, the first-order question of the nature of security is firmly on the political agenda. As a consequence, the role of military force – for so long central to perceptions of security – is uncertain. The question is no longer how much military power is required for security; rather it is the relationship between military power and security.

This chapter argues that challenges to the centrality of military power to security pre-dated the end of the Cold War. In the 1980s a series of ideas were developed which began to reformulate traditional views concerning security and the utility of military power. In post-Cold War Europe, these challenges may help to form a new security agenda. Alternatively, the new security structure may reinforce old ideas about the utility of military power. This chapter therefore begins with an analysis of the first order question of the nature of security and the role of military power in security. It examines the traditional, Cold War perspective on this issue, and the challenges to this orthodoxy which emerged in the 1980s. It then examines the role of military power in post-Cold War Europe in the light of this, and specifically how military power might be managed in post-Cold War Europe.

SECURITY AND MILITARY FORCE

For most academic strategists and policy-makers during the Cold War, the nature of security was unproblematic. Security was seen largely, sometimes exclusively, in military terms. Peace, moreover, was seen simply as the absence of war. Thus for the west peace and security required the absence of war with the Soviet Union, a view which led inevitably to strategies of deterrence and to a reliance on nuclear weapons. For some forty years therefore deterrence occupied a position of unchallenged centrality both in the academic discipline of strategic studies and in the defence policy of western states. Indeed at times deterrence appeared to be more than merely the 'jewel in the crown' of strategic studies (Booth 1987: 254); to all intents and purposes it was strategic studies, and the maintenance of credible deterrence was the major task of western security policy (Gray 1982; HMSO 1987: 13–14). The centrality of deterrence to western security policy was therefore a product of the particular view of security promoted during the Cold War: that peace and security came from the absence of war with the Soviet Union, and that a credible deterrent was the best means of preventing war from occurring (McInnes 1991: 1–2).

During the Cold War a high value was also placed on stability as an important element in the effective working of deterrence. Classical deterrence theory saw stability in largely technical terms – the preservation of retaliatory capabilities in the face of technological breakthroughs or an increase in the enemy's military arsenal (Wohlstetter 1959). But it was also apparent that deterrence worked best in conditions of political stability. Political stability enabled a clear dividing line to be drawn between friend and enemy (what alternative defence theorists sometimes criticised as 'enemy imaging'). Political stability facilitated bloc loyalty, or bloc hegemony. And political stability allowed the area over which the deterrent umbrella was spread to be clearly drawn. Thus stability was highly prized, both in terms of weapons development and political order.

Finally, since deterrence relied on devastating firepower, nuclear weapons rose in prominence until they became the central weapons of western security policy. Although nuclear weapons constituted a relatively small proportion of defence budgets, and a similarly small percentage of the number of weapons available to military planners, they dominated both academic thinking and military planning in the Cold War. In particular nuclear weapons assisted in the creation of deterrence strategies through their awesome destructive power – conventional weapons, though enormously destructive, did not possess the same world-shattering potential. As the 1987 British Defence White Paper stated:

NATO could not achieve such deterrence by conventional weapons alone. An adversary who no longer faced the risk of nuclear retaliation might once again regard force as a usable option, since the costs of aggression might no longer be prohibitively high.

(HMSO 1987: 13)

But equally if not more importantly, their destructive power made war unthinkable and so forced deterrence upon military planners. In Bernard Brodie's famous words:

Thus far the chief purpose of our military establishments has been to win wars. From now on it must be to avert them. It can have almost no other useful purpose.

(Brodie 1946: 76)

The relationship between nuclear weapons and deterrence therefore resembled that of the chicken and the egg: deterrence required the destructive power of nuclear weapons to create a sufficient threat to deter, while the same destructive power made warfare less attractive as a policy option, and therefore led to policies of deterrence.[1]

Thus Cold War strategists saw security in terms of a military response to a military threat. The chief aims of security policy were peace and stability, peace being defined as the absence of war. To achieve peace and stability strategies emphasised the deterrence of war by nuclear threats rather than the ability to defend territory through war-fighting capabilities. This in turn was influenced by the destructive power of nuclear weapons, which made fighting a war 'unthinkable'. Security institutions similarly reflected this military bias. The North Atlantic Treaty Organisation (NATO), the Warsaw Pact and the Western European Union (WEU) were all predominantly, if not exclusively military organisations, while other institutions such as the pan-European Conference on Security and Cooperation in Europe (CSCE) had a heavy military bias. In contrast the major west European economic (and, increasingly, political) institution, the European Community (EC) explicitly denied itself a security role during the Cold War.

By the 1980s however this perspective was increasingly being challenged. Three main challenges can be identified: first, the emergence of a broadened security agenda; secondly, the development of ideas of common security, initially developed by alternative defence theorists in the west, but also advocated by Soviet President Mikhail Gorbachev in the late 1980s; and finally a growing awareness of the reduced value of military power in international relations, and in particular the reduced utility of military force in Europe. To a certain extent these ideas were linked – at the very least they were mutually reinforcing. But the important point is that by the end of the 1980s, and before the revolutions of 1989–91, the orthodox view of security was under sustained pressure from both policy-makers and academic analysts, and the consensus over the nature of security looked increasingly fragile.

The first of these challenges concerned the emergence of a broadened security agenda. Cold War security tended to be a minimalist concept: the defence of the state against external aggression. Security was viewed at the level of the state – hence the common usage of the term 'national security' – and involved the use of military power to deter or repel aggression. But this appeared increasingly unsatisfactory both in terms of the level at which security was considered, and the range of threats addressed. Security was not just a problem for the state, but for individuals within a state suffering repression, oppression or a denial of basic human rights. For many, the major threat to their security concerned the repression of individual freedoms and rights – limitations on democracy, freedom of assembly, free speech, the rule of law, etc. Security was a matter of threats to the individual, not just to the state (see Part I). Indeed the state could all too easily become the security problem, particularly if it subjugated human rights to narrowly defined state interests (what is usually termed 'state security'). In these circumstances human rights were repressed for the sake of the state: state interests were paramount, and because individual free-doms might challenge this they were to be repressed. This situation was all too common in eastern Europe during the Cold War, but was also not entirely alien to the west (Fritzsche 1989: 52–3; Gerle 1989: 376; Kaldor 1989: 62–3; Ponting 1985: 205–14).

During the 1980s therefore individual security and human rights came increasingly to be seen as important security concerns, and as a legitimate part of the debate on security. Security did not apply to merely the state, but to individuals whose security might be threatened by the state. But the widening of the security agenda did not stop there. At the other end of the scale global security concerns began to emerge over issues such as the environment and the proliferation of weapons of mass destruction. It was clear that the effects of an environmental catastrophe such as ozone depletion and global warming went beyond the boundaries of individual states; nor were such problems soluble at the level of states in Europe, requiring instead an unprecedented degree of international cooperation. As George Robertson commented:

There is no sovereignty in Westminster over acid rain, or over radioactive fallout from Chernobyl or the decisions of major companies. When money markets cross over national boundaries at will there is precious little sovereignty left over key economic areas.

(Robertson 1990: 699)

Such concerns threaten life, lifestyle and livelihood. They are therefore security concerns. But the state has little or no control over them. Thus a third level of security emerged – that of global security.

During the 1980s therefore a movement was discernible whereby the levels at which security was considered were broadened. The traditional narrow focus on the state was expanded to a more 'holistic' conception involving individual and global concerns as well as national (Buzan 1983; 1991). In addition, and closely related to this, the range of issues considered as security concerns broadened. Whereas security was traditionally viewed as an almost exclusively military concern, during the 1980s other issues began to appear on the security agenda. Economic issues had long been accepted as being related to security – Duncan Sandys' 1957 defence review in the UK was but one example whereby defence spending was cut for fear of distorting the nation's welfare. But in the 1980s the link was made somewhat more explicit, and rather more fundamental. Economic issues were not merely security issues in that they affected lifestyle, livelihood and *in extremis* life (reflecting in turn the growing awareness of individual security concerns), but because economic prosperity produced satisfaction and stability, contributing towards security at the state (i.e., international) level. Economic issues affected individual security through their impact upon individual well-being – standards of living, security of employment, housing and shelter, access to food and other essentials. But economic issues could also affect international security in that prosperous, economically satisfied states were less likely to be aggressive and upset the status quo.

Secondly, as environmental concerns began to force their way into mainstream political consciousness, so an awareness developed of the security implications of environmental change. The initial tendency perhaps was to see environmental change as producing security problems – that drought, for example, might produce migration (Brown 1989: 528). But increasingly the environment has been seen as a security issue in its own right, by threatening life, lifestyle and livelihood; both at the level of the individual and of the state (see Chapter 7). Finally, given the increased awareness of individual security concerns, so human rights came to figure more prominently on the security agenda. Though human rights had been related to security concerns in the past (notably through the CSCE process), the relationship tended often to be rhetorical and peripheral rather than central and substantive. During the 1980s human rights increasingly came to be seen as a legitimate security issue in their own right, and a central component in individual security (see Chapter 8).

The 1980s therefore saw a challenge to the stranglehold military power had traditionally exerted over the security agenda. Economic issues, human rights and environmental concerns all began to emerge as legitimate security concerns. Further, whereas security had traditionally resided in the state, a more holistic view began to be developed whereby the state constituted just one level of security, with individual and global security concerns not merely robbing the state of its monopoly on security, but even threatening the state's centrality in thinking about security.

A second challenge to the relationship between military power and security came through the development of ideas concerning common security. This approach suggested that security could not be achieved by unilateral means, but only by cooperation on issues of mutual concern (Vayrynan 1985). The implications of this for the relationship between military power and security were three-fold. First, it suggested that unilateral attempts at security by military means were counterproductive. The key analytical tool behind this was the security dilemma (Jervis 1978). The security dilemma argued that in a confrontational situation, unilateral attempts to increase military security would be perceived as threatening by an opponent. The opponent would then take countervailing measures, fuelling the arms race. No military advantage would accrue, while tensions would be increased. Thus security could actually be reduced by unilateral attempts to gain military advantage. Secondly, common security presented a case that security was much more dependent upon political rather than military factors – an idea which figured prominently in President Gorbachev's 'new thinking' on security in the late 1980s (Meyer 1989). According to this view, the balance of military forces was less important for security in Europe than the political relationship between the two blocs.

Finally, common security challenged the 'zero-sum' thinking of orthodox strategists. Implicit – and sometimes explicit – in much of the security thinking of the Cold War was the idea that a development which was of advantage to one side would be disadvantageous to the other (Freedman 1989: 182–9; Kaplan 1983: 63–8). Thus the deployment of SS20s in the 1970s for example was advantageous to the Soviets and equally disadvantageous to NATO. Through the workings of the security dilemma, however, the eventual result was not one of Soviet advantage but of mutual disadvantage: NATO deployed cruise missiles and Pershing II to offset the Soviet advantage of the SS20, leading to a deterioration in political relations and in overall security. Thus in practice zero-sum game thinking resulted in a negative-sum game. Common security, however, advocated a positive-sum game – in other words that security should be approached from the perspective not of seeking unilateral advantage, but from one of mutual benefit (Booth 1990). The implication behind common security was that military power alone could not ensure security, rather that security should be based on a cooperative approach to constrain and regulate military power.

Thus the development of ideas of common security constituted a second challenge to the orthodox view of the relationship between security and military power. The final challenge, however, concerned the very utility of military power in Europe. The cost of war in Europe had clearly increased from a number of perspectives. Most obviously the destructive capabilities of modern weapons are so great that, even if they were used in a primarily counterforce manner, the devastation caused might pose questions over the utility of war. But the danger is that once one side began to lose so it might escalate the conflict by shifting away from targetting military forces and towards targetting civilian and industrial centres. In so doing it would have less to lose than the other side, while escalation might create pressure for a ceasefire or even succeed in reversing the fortunes of war. (It should be noted that this argument applies to conventional as well as nuclear forces, given the destructive power of modern conventional weapons.) The consequence is therefore that the devastation likely to be caused by a war in Europe would act as a major disincentive to using military power. In addition the economic and financial costs of war, both in terms of the cost of military operations and the economic dislocation involved, along with the human and (increasingly) the environmental costs of war, are now so great as to provide further major disincentives to using military power. Finally war may lead to international political pressure on the state (as the Soviets experienced in Afghanistan and the Iraqis in Kuwait), domestic discontent, and even social change in a state, the latter two being particularly likely if the war goes badly (as was the case with Argentina in the Falklands/Malvinas war). Therefore the potential political costs of using military power are very high.

In addition to the high cost of war acting as a disincentive, the incentives to using military power in Europe appeared to be substantially reduced in the 1980s. In particular the potential gains from aggression appeared to be diminishing as west European economies moved into a post-industrial phase. In this phase the physical resources of a state (raw materials, plant, labour, etc.) are less important than its creative resources and the network of communications. Eastern Europe failed economically not because of a lack of productive resources, but because of a lack of creative resources and limitations upon communication and exchange of ideas. The repressive domestic structures of the former Communist east at best provided no incentive for innovation, and at worst stifled it. In crude but none the less telling terms, while West Germany produced BMWs and Mercedes, East Germany produced the Trabant. This inability to compete because of the stifling of innovation was clearly reflected by the introduction of perestroika and glasnost in the Soviet Union in an attempt to reinvigorate the Soviet economy by loosening oppressive central control. The development of post-industrial societies has a major implication for the utility of military force. An aggressor would have to suppress opposition in an invaded state, but in so doing would be unable to exploit its creative resources. Aggression would therefore appear to offer fewer benefits than in the past, suggesting that not only have the costs of war increased, but that the potential gains have been significantly reduced.

None of this meant that military power could not be used in Europe. Nor indeed did it mean that circumstances could no longer arise when military force represented an attractive and rational policy option. But these occasions were likely to be fewer, and the attraction of military force substantially reduced by these developments. War was still a policy option, and military force still had its uses. But the likelihood of military power being used in Europe at the interstate level appeared increasingly remote.

During the 1980s therefore the traditional relationship between security and military power was challenged on a number of grounds. In particular the idea of military power being just one of a number of issues on the security agenda, and that of a more holistic, less state-centric approach to security began to receive considerable interest. By the time of the revolutionary changes of 1989–91 however it was far from clear whether these challenges had acquired a critical mass of support, and whether the orthodoxy was close to being overthrown. What was clear though was that the consensus over the relationship between security and military power had been shattered. What remained to be seen was whether post-Cold War Europe would support the challengers, or whether it would reassert orthodoxy; whether the new Europe would offer a reduced role for military concerns and a broadened security agenda, or whether 'power politics' would be reasserted and military power resume centre stage in security debates.

SECURITY AND MILITARY POWER IN POST-COLD WAR EUROPE

The answer to this question appears to be mixed. The threat of a major war involving the entire continent has clearly receded with the collapse first of the Warsaw Pact and then of the Soviet Union. Similarly the threat of interstate conflict is almost unimaginable in western Europe. But in eastern Europe, southern Europe and the former Soviet Union it is difficult to be so optimistic. Two major problems are apparent. The first concerns the unsatisfactory, unclear and/or contentious nature of many of the international boundaries in these areas. Most were decided in the aftermath of the Second World War, and reflect the political and security concerns of that era. Today many are at best anachronistic and at worst capable of producing a highly volatile confrontation. Secondly, and related to this, state boundaries do not necessarily coincide with national groupings. Thus a state may find that a large number of its 'people' in cultural and national terms are citizens of a neighbouring state where they constitute an ethnic minority. If this ethnic minority feels threatened – rightly or wrongly – then its links with the friendly neighbouring state may lead to interstate tension. Thus the position of the Turkish minority in Bulgaria for example, and that of the Armenian enclave in Azerbaijan has created tensions which might in turn lead to interstate conflict.

In addition to this increased risk of interstate conflict, the risk of internal conflict has also grown substantially. Again there appear to be two potential causes for this. The first is the danger that weak domestic political structures will be unable to mediate between political groupings (Snyder 1990). Events in Georgia in early 1992 have already demonstrated how the transition from communism to other forms of political structure may lead to violent confrontations between groups competing for legitimacy and power. New political structures may lack the respect or the power to act as a source of authority within the state. In these situations disaffected groups may turn to violence as a means not simply of airing grievances but of effecting political change. Secondly, ethnic minorities which see themselves as persecuted and/or desire independence may use violence as a means towards their own political ends. Alternatively, they may find violence used against them by the central governing authority in order to suppress dissent. The conflict in former Yugoslavia is perhaps the clearest example of this latter danger.

Military force has also seen its stock rise in the wake of Operation Desert Shield/Storm. In particular the success of coalition operations, and the media's extensive coverage of the war has created an image of the utility of military power. Whether such intervention will become the norm – that the west's military forces will find a role policing a 'new world order' – appears somewhat unlikely, but similar operations cannot be ruled out in the future. More importantly perhaps the Gulf War may act as a totem, asserting that military power may still need to be called upon in the future, when it will once more play a central role in world events. It reminded people that, despite an optimistic turn of events in Europe, the world remained a dangerous place – in the words of General Colin Powell, 'there is the enduring reality of the unknown, of a world that continues to harbour danger, uncertainty and instability' (Powell 1991: 19). As a result strong military power may prove essential to the protection of legitimate security interests. But perhaps what matters most here is less the likelihood of a repeat performance in the Gulf or elsewhere than the psychological impact caused by military operations in the Gulf: that soldiers, politicians and the public saw military force being used, and being used very successfully by the west. Thus the perception of the utility of military force was clearly affected by the events in the Gulf.

The Second Gulf War therefore had two distinct impacts. The first was on the public perception of the utility of military force. To deny the utility of military force in the wake of Operation Desert Storm was to invite at best incredulity and at worst ridicule. Whether this perception will last for long is unclear. Certainly the political popularity George Bush derived from the Second Gulf War was short lived. Secondly, events in the Gulf raised the question of the utility of military force for intervening in 'out of area' (i.e., extra European) disputes where western interests might be at risk (Foot 1992). Certainly post-Cold War US military reorganization suggests that intervention and force projection is seen in Washington as an important military task for the future (*Independent* 1992; *Jane's Defence Weekly* 1992, 1992a).[2] But enthusiasm in Europe for this sort of venture is somewhat less than wholehearted, while the question of intervention in a European dispute appears to have considerably less support – suggestions in 1991 that the WEU might intervene in the former Yugoslav civil war received short shrift (see Chapter 8). Even the question of peacekeeping seems to be outside European hands – not least due to the political sensitivities of a European force being involved in a European dispute, but also due to a lack of institutional machinery.

So what does all of this suggest about the utility of military force? It is perhaps useful to distinguish here between use and utility. Certainly military force has been used, and may be used more frequently after the end of the Cold War than in the period immediately preceding 1989. This tends to suggest that military security will become more important. What is unclear, however, is how useful military force is likely to be in Europe. The potential for interstate violence may be higher than during the Cold War, but that does not mean that the powerful disincentives to the use of military force which were outlined in the previous section will be easily overridden. To state that the end of the Cold War has 'taken the lid off' a variety of interstate disputes which are now likely to boil over is too simplistic. It assumes that bloc loyalty (or bloc hegemony) was the sole reason for the lack of interstate conflicts within blocs. It ignores other disincentives to war which remain despite the collapse of the blocs and the ending of the Cold War, particularly the high cost of war. This is not to say that interstate violence cannot and will not happen. It is rather to say that the utility of military force at the interstate level is still questionable, and may therefore act as a powerful disincentive to war.

The case of military power within states appears somewhat clearer, however. The handful of conflicts which have already occurred are overshadowed by the potential number lurking in the wings. The civil war in former Yugoslavia may be the harbinger of many such conflicts, particularly in the former Soviet Union. Not only do these conflicts appear more likely in post-Cold War Europe, the utility of military force is often seen as much greater here than at the interstate level: low intensity violence is commonly used by insurgent groupings, while military power is an equally common response by governments to quell disturbances, from the British in Northern Ireland to the Soviets in Nagorno Karabakh. Whether military power can satisfactorily resolve these disputes is unclear. But what is clear is that military power is seen as essential in managing and controlling these disputes, and that it comes to dominate the security agenda in these situations.

Finally, despite its success in the Second Gulf War, intervention seems unlikely to become commonplace in Europe due to political sensitivities and its high cost. Moreover, gaining the moral authority and cohesive political support for intervention, factors which were such necessary preconditions for the political success of Operation Desert Storm, is likely to be much more difficult in Europe. Indeed the civil war in former Yugoslavia has shown how difficult even peacekeeping operations can be on a purely European basis. This may change over time, and the CSCE may develop the necessary machinery for peacekeeping, but in the meantime neither intervention nor peacekeeping is likely to figure prominently in intra-European security policies.

If the question of the utility of military power in post-Cold War Europe produces a mixed answer, that concerning the broadened security agenda appears somewhat more certain. The dominance that military issues exerted over the security agenda has been challenged and its grip broken. Economic issues have clearly achieved a new prominence: instability and insecurity in eastern and southern Europe and the former Soviet Union are clearly related to the economic problems currently being experienced by former communist states. Economic problems may not be the sole source of insecurity there, but they are clearly an important, if not the single most important, security problem. This situation has been recognised in the west with its commitment to economic aid for these states. This aid is not simple altruism – though it would be ungracious to deny the very real feelings of sympathy and desire to help relieve human suffering there. Rather it is based upon the realisation that economic problems in the former Communist states affect not merely the security of individuals in those states, but the security of Europe as a whole. Western security is dependent upon stability in the east, which in turn is closely related to its economic well being.

Similarly environmental issues are beginning to figure more prominently on the international agenda – even to the extent of appearing on the agenda of the G7's (seven leading industrial powers) 1991 summit in London. Though press reports suggested that environmental issues actually received little attention in the summit (*The Independent*, 1991), the fact that they were placed on the agenda at all suggests a growing awareness of environmental issues. Finally, human rights were at the heart of the revolutions of 1989–91, with issues such as free speech, freedom of association, pluralism and democratic accountability high on the list of popular demands. The process of implementing these changes and of setting them in robust political structures has not been easy, and in some states reforms have been less than entirely convincing (Romania and Bulgaria, for example). Moreover, the problem of minority rights is likely to recur on a regular basis, particularly with the large number of ethnic minorities in eastern and southern Europe and the former Soviet Union. Human rights therefore emerged as a security issue in 1989–91, and is likely to retain this position as the process of reform is worked through, and as questions of minority rights continue to recur.

In addition to new issues challenging the centrality of military power to the post-Cold War security agenda, the state's position as the locus of security has also been challenged. Human rights have most obviously placed individual security concerns high on the political agenda. At the system level though, developments have also been apparent. First, there has been a growing awareness of the interdependence of security issues – military, economic and environmental. Perhaps the most startling development has been in the military field where disarmament – unilateral and multilateral, nuclear and conventional – has displaced arms control. Building down through disarmament is seen as reducing tensions, reflecting the interdependence of military security. Secondly, at the institutional level the old alliance structures are fading and are being replaced by other bodies, particularly the CSCE, the WEU and the EC's nascent Common Foreign and Security Policy (CFSP). The most interesting of these are the developments within the EC, because what a CFSP proposes is less an alliance and more a harmonisation of policies leading eventually to integration into a supranational security policy. In the 1980s this was little more than a pipe dream; in the 1990s it is a realistic possibility.

What does this mean for military security in the new Europe? The development of a broader agenda suggests that military issues will become less central to security concerns, but equally the possibility of interstate conflict is real, while internal conflict is likely. Military security cannot therefore be ignored, but neither should it dominate the security debate as it did during the Cold War. How then should military security be managed in post-Cold War Europe?

THE MANAGEMENT OF MILITARY SECURITY

The management of military security has two aspects. The first concerns policies to meet threats and risks to security, the second concerns institutions. To deal with the second aspect first, four main institutions appear to have survived the Cold War and may play a role in the future of European Security: NATO, the WEU, the CSCE and the EC. Whether these institutions are in competition with each other, or whether they can complement each other is unclear. The WEU, for example, has been seen as complementary to the EC, but in other respects it may be in competition with NATO. The role of these institutions may be portrayed in terms of overlapping circles of interest – that each institution covers certain areas and membership patterns, some of which may be unique to that institution but others may be shared with one or more other institutions. This analogy is helpful in portraying the degree of overlap in terms of interests coupled to the uniqueness of each institution. But it implies that this provides a satisfactory coverage of security issues within a framework of complementary institutions. In fact the coverage is far from satisfactory (the lack of a major institution explicitly concerned with environmental security, for example, appears a major deficiency), and the degree of overlap has yet to be codified into a complementary system, and may still prove to be confused and competitive.

This is most obvious in the military field where the role of all four institutions remains unclear. Despite movement towards a CFSP, the EC remains plagued by doubts and problems over military cooperation; the CSCE encountered difficulties in moving from a negotiating body to one with a more proactive role; the WEU has a somewhat unclear relationship with NATO and the EC; while NATO has yet to find a credible role to ensure its survival as a pivotal force in European security. This uncertainty means that there is no clear framework of institutions with clearly defined roles and functions to provide security – particularly military security – in Europe. Moreover, there is a distinct possibility that as the remaining institutions develop, so they may find themselves in competition with other institutions for particular roles. At risk is not merely the credibility and survival of these institutions, but effective management of security issues if states are divided over the institutions best placed to serve particular needs.

One other point is worth noting concerning these security institutions. None of them are new bodies, all being products in some form or other of the Cold War. That they were created to satisfy the requirements of the Cold War does not necessarily mean that they are inappropriate for post-Cold War Europe, but it does raise questions over their future relevance. In response all four institutions have been evolving, though some more successfully than others. NATO has been attempting to develop more of a political focus, though it has failed to expand its membership beyond its Cold War origins. The WEU has been attempting to raise its profile as a distinctively European military institution, and may act as a bridge between NATO and the EC, or indeed may become the military arm of the EC; but this rather confused state of affairs tends to suggest that the current nature of the WEU is highly unsatisfactory (RUSI 1991). The CSCE has been attempting to gain a more active role in European security, and particularly in conflict management, but appears to be severely handicapped by the general requirement for unanimity in its decision-making. Finally, the EC is edging towards a common military policy as part of CFSP, but the process is not set in concrete and given the number of problems likely to be encountered may easily be derailed. Therefore this evolutionary process has yet to realise a satisfactory outcome, while no new institution has emerged to manage military security in Europe.

The second major aspect of the management of military security concerns strategies and policies adopted to meet threats and risks in post-Cold War Europe. It is perhaps worth noting the semantic sea change which has occurred since 1989–91. 'Threats' are passé, being too closely associated with the Cold War image of the Soviet 'threat'. Rather military planners talk increasingly in terms of 'risks'. That this is largely a western development serves to underline the manner in which the security debate can be – and often is – dominated by the western perspective. For policy planners in the west there is no clear military threat to plan against. Rather there are a number of often ill-defined risks. The vagueness of risks rather than threats makes planning difficult. As a result flexibility, and in particular the ability to meet and react to a wide variety of possible scenarios is often emphasised. But equally apparent is the way in which NATO strategy has remained relatively unchanged by these developments. Its Cold War hallmarks of a willingness to escalate, a reliance on nuclear weapons (albeit now somewhat reduced), and the reliance on heavy armour and airpower for conventional defence remain very much in evidence even after the ending of the Cold War (Baylis 1992; Croft 1992). The difficulty in planning for post-Cold War Europe has therefore led to two identifiable trends in the west: an emphasis upon flexibility, and the continued development of existing strategic approaches rather than creating radical new ones.

In eastern Europe the situation is somewhat more confused, not least as a result of the fragmentation of the Warsaw Pact and of individual states (most notably the Soviet Union and Yugoslavia). Nevertheless, three trends are apparent. The first is towards an ostensibly defensive defence policy, a policy which is orientated purely towards the defence of the state rather than an 'offensive' defence policy or an intervention capability. Secondly, and related to this, is an acceptance of reasonable sufficiency. In contrast to the old Soviet stereotype of 'too much is never enough', post-Cold War eastern Europe appears to be emphasising restraint in the size of armed forces, both as a means of alleviating international tension, but perhaps more importantly out of economic necessity (RUSI 1991a). Finally, there is a marked reluctance to establish a new military security structure to replace the Warsaw Pact, and consequently an increased emphasis upon national self-sufficiency. Even in the Commonwealth of Independent States (CIS), the future of a unified military force is uncertain, and states are developing national military structures of their own. Although a number of east European states have expressed an interest in joining NATO, at present the door appears firmly shut, and states are thrown back on their own resources.

CONCLUSION

In conclusion then there appears to be some lack of clarity over military security in post-Cold War Europe. Security policies and institutions are still evolving, while the apparent increase in the use of military force is offset by continued doubts over its utility in international politics. Perhaps most important, however, is the movement away from a minimalist view of security in which military concerns were dominant, and towards a broader security agenda. This movement is far from complete, but substantial progress has been made along this path, and the unchallenged supremacy of military issues in security policies may now be a thing of the past.

NOTES

1   It should be noted that deterrence does not necessarily rely on nuclear weapons, merely that nuclear weapons provided sufficient firepower to create a credible deterrent threat. The classic study of non-nuclear deterrence is J. Mearsheimer (1983) *Conventional Deterrence*.

2   The Pentagon has drawn up a list of seven possible wars which it might have to fight in the next decade, and is basing its plans upon a capability to fight at least two regional wars simultaneously, or to meet the challenge of a new expansionist superpower (referred to as REGT – Resurgent / Emergent Global Threat).

Chapter 6

The economic agenda
R. J. Barry Jones

INTRODUCTION

The future evolution of Europe turns around developments at four levels of activity – the regional, the state, the Community and the global – and within three increasingly inter-related spheres of action – the existing European Community (EC), the wider western Europe, and Continental Europe in general. Tensions amongst these levels and spheres of activity generate a range of uncertainties about the direction and rate of future European developments.

While the EC was the creature of its initial member states, its further development and consolidation poses threats to the authority, and even the survival, of the very states that gave it birth. Substate regions challenge some established states. The EC is also troubled by the possibilities of further expansion: initially to incorporate the members of the European Free Trade Area (EFTA); and latterly, perhaps, to absorb many of the states on its eastern frontiers. Such expansion will fulfil much of the Community's promise as a solution to many of the historical problems of conflict and economic fragmentation, but bring with it increased problems of control and cohesiveness.

Europe's current relations with the wider world also encompass inconsistencies and uncertainties. A nominal commitment to a liberal international economic order fits uneasily with the neo-mercantilist features of many of the EC's established, and emergent, policies and programmes. The growth of interest in a European-based security structure also discords with, yet may be encouraged by, a vision of a new international order led by a predominant United States of America.

Whatever the ultimate resolution of such tensions, the economic development of Europe is of central significance to the contemporary international political economy. Europe's future relations with the USA, Japan, the states of the Pacific Rim, and the Third World are central to the prospects of each. Within Europe itself, the central factor is the existence, further development and regional impact of the EC.

By the mid-1980s the twelve member states of the EC accounted for some 57 per cent of world exports and 52.9 per cent of imports (Harrop 1989: 169, Table 9.1), or some 21 per cent of exports and 22 per cent of imports when world trade is calculated by excluding trade amongst the EC's members (Barnes 1988: 44, Table 4.1). The comparative shares of world exports and imports (excluding intra-EC trade) of the USA were 15 per cent and 21 per cent; and those of Japan 11 per cent and 9 per cent (Barnes 1988: 44). The EC, as an entity, thus constitutes the strongest trading presence on the world stage. An economic actor of such magnitude cannot be ignored by any members of the international economic community. Its influence upon its neighbours can be vortical: drawing inwards those in close proximity; slewing off those at greater cultural, economic and geographical distance.

The character and ultimate impact of the EC remains, however, a matter of considerable controversy. The path of economic integration within western Europe since the formation of the European Coal and Steel Community (ECSC) in 1952 can be seen in varying lights. While the EC has often been depicted as an inevitable consequence of compulsive forces towards economic integration and rationalisation in an ever more complex and competitive world economy, the promotion of economic integration has sometimes been dubbed a politically motivated stratagem for fomenting a new European political identity of sufficient strength and coherence to exert a new, and forceful, presence upon the world stage. In its impact upon the world economy, the EC has, at times, been heralded as a stepping-stone to a fully liberalised global trading system; at other times condemned as a protectionist pariah. The cohesiveness and robustness of the EC experiment has also been viewed from contrasting perspectives: some perceiving an irresistible force and logic in its continued development; others identifying a multitude of fragmentary and centrifugal forces that might yet tear the adolescent community asunder.

While many questions of interpretation and explanation will remain controversial, a number of recent developments have provided evidence of the momentum now attained by the process of integration within Europe and indications of the kind of impact that the EC will have upon world affairs in the foreseeable future.

EUROPEAN INTEGRATION: BEYOND THE CRITICAL THRESHOLD OF INTEGRATION?

There are now signs that the movement towards deeper and wider European integration may have passed a critical threshold, and attained a clear integrative momentum. Advance throughout the 1970s and early 1980s was often slow. The signature of the European Single Act of 1986, heralding the creation of a single market by the end of 1992 (*The Economist* 1988), signalled a major resurgence of interest in further economic integration and, as witnessed by its adoption of qualified majority voting on many aspects of its implementation, the development of corresponding political structures. The depth and durability of this commitment was demonstrated by its survival through the political crisis precipitated by the Iraqi invasion of Kuwait and the damaging divisions over the appropriate response.

The EC's attractive force is evidenced in Great Britain's accession to the Single European Act and by its adherence, rhetoric aside, to the majority of subsequent EC agreements of substance; in the dramatic surge of interest in closer association amongst non-EC European states, whether they be members of EFTA or former satellites of the Soviet Union in central, eastern and south-eastern Europe. Such interest has found tangible expression in the succession of new applications for admission to the EC and the agreement in principle of October 1991 to encompass the members of the EC and EFTA within a new European Economic Area (EEA).

The EC has now established itself as the representative of all its member states in wider negotiations on trade issues, whether they be at the Uruguay Round negotiations of the General Agreement on Tariffs and Trade (GATT) or the agreement of quotas on vehicle imports into the Community from Japan. Practically, the EC also confronts the rest of the world with the levies imposed under the Common Agricultural Policy (CAP) and the Common External Tariff on other imported goods and commodities.

The development of the EC has also interacted with global developments. Regional integration within Europe may be stimulating a response in kind within other regions of the world economy. Within Europe, the progress of the 1992 project has reinforced inclinations towards regional association more widely within the continent (*The Economist* 1991c). As ambivalence towards the European project has shaded into anxiety elsewhere, increasing interest has been shown in the creation of the North American Free Trade Area, and the prospects for economic free trade areas within southern Latin America and south-east Asia.[1] Grumbling anxieties have also stimulated concerns amongst US political leaders about the longer-term strategic posture of Europe (*The Guardian* 1991b).

THE IMPULSES FOR EUROPEAN INTEGRATION: CONVIVIAL COMMUNITY OR 'FORTRESS EUROPE'?

Many of the early motives for European integration reflected recent historical experiences. A Europe riven by two catastrophic conflagrations within a mere half century was a fertile breeding ground for aspirations for a better, and more secure, future. The formal association of, and integration amongst, the Continent's historic belligerents offered an attractive alternative to Europe's self-immolatory impulses (Gladwyn 1966). The need for economic reconstruction, and substantial rationalisation, was also pressing during the early post-Second World War years.

External forces also reinforced impulses towards European integration. The USA and the USSR had usurped the historically dominant position of Europe's leading states within world affairs. The pressures of growing economic competition were also felt, first from the USA, then Japan and latterly the Newly Industrialised Countries (NICs). Such developments gradually generated a perceived reality of regional competition, which challenged the loose rhetoric of international economic interdependence and encouraged interest in further European regionalisation.[2] It is thus entirely possible that, as even free trade proponents have been forced to admit (*The Economist* 1989a) economic policy and activity will become more intensely focused within increasingly differentiated regions of the world economy. Europe, in such a new order, would provide a stronger and more effective basis for the neo-mercantilist competition amongst the worlds major regional economic blocs.

Arguments that membership of the EC was necessary and 'inevitable' for a succession of new member states sustained the continued expansion of the Community and the increase of its economic strength and impact; endowing the EC with an ever-increasing centripetal force. With the conclusion of the Single European Act and the approach of January 1993, prospects of exclusion from an increasingly self-regarding EC economy and proto-state have exercised the minds of many on the borders of the EC. Centripetal pressures have prompted changes of views about association with, and possible membership of, the EC. Such considerations were exemplified by the October 1991 announcement of the combination of the EC and EFTA within a new European Economic Area embracing some 380 million citizens and generating some 46 per cent of world trade (*The Economist* 1991f) Moreover, all the members of EFTA have now either declared a wish to join the EC or are known, as in Norway's case, to be reviewing former reservations. The long-held neutrality of such a reluctant debutante as Austria is now no longer deemed to be a serious obstacle to eventual membership of the EC. The newly liberated states of central and eastern Europe have also formed a queue to secure association with the EC and to establish the principle of ultimate, albeit much delayed, full membership.

An emergent Euro-region might assume distinct structural characteristics. A slowly expanding, but ever-deepening, core of full members of the European Community being surrounded by an outer ring of associated states, steadily pursuing economic, social and political convergence with the core. Beyond its periphery of European associates, the Euro-region might maintain loose, although often uneasy, relations with a set of semi-client states within the African, Caribbean and Pacific Group (ACP). However, it is possible that this relationship will shrink to a cosmetic residue with the further progress of economic regionalisation and European integration.

The prospects of the further enlargement of the EC will merely compound the challenges of diversity. The structure and functioning of the EFTA states is sufficiently congruent with that of the leading members of the current EC to ensure a relatively easy process of assimilation. The strains attendant upon the possible accession of many of the states of central and eastern Europe, however, present a far less sanguine picture. Substantial levels of economic convergence with the Community will have to be achieved before the transition to full membership can be attempted with any confidence. Such convergence will, however, be promoted through the assistance provided via the new, London based, European Bank for Reconstruction and Development (EBRD), the EC's *ad hoc* relief programmes, the aid efforts of the EC's individual states and the granting of associate status to promising central and eastern European economies.

The politico-economic dilemmas for Europe are at their sharpest in central and eastern Europe. Left to their own devices, much of the region threatens to descend into economic chaos and to germinate divisive, and ultimately lethal, political passions. The impact of such disruptive developments is of general concern to the European Community and worries many of its individual members. The concerns of individual member states vary according to differences in geopolitical conditions. The Community's more eastern members fear the direct consequences of disorders on their frontiers. More distanced Community states are more exercised by the prospects of a re-emergent strategic threat. All, however, are anxious about the prospects of mass migrations of peoples displaced by protracted disorder

or economic breakdown within the eastern 'marches'. Political considerations thus overlay purely economic calculations about the desirability of
the further enlargement of the EC. Considerations of security, sentiment
and longer-term strategic regional strength will caution against the outright
rejection of a number of otherwise problematic applicants, despite the
problems of diversity that, as has been considered elsewhere, such expansion would entail.

The island states of the Mediterranean, Cyprus and Malta, are also
engaged in the slow process of converting associate status into full membership. The EC's calculations of the economic consequences of admission
are complicated by a sense of these states' participation in a common
European heritage and of their potential salience to Europe's future security
and stability. Here, the contrast is sharp with the case of Turkey, whose
application for consideration for full membership continues to meet with
sustained official equivocation.

For states and societies that ultimately find themselves excluded from
admission to the European club the consequences could be severe. Denied
more than mere associate status, or the weak links of the Lomé Conventions, excluded states in eastern and central Europe, or amongst the
Community's associates within the Third World, will remain supplicants
at the European economic feast rather than full participants. In the
'worst-case' scenario, such states might be condemned to languish on the
margins of an ever-more prosperous Europe, while the global political
economy assumes an increasingly regionalised structure. Costly and complex efforts to establish wider economic links would constitute the only
alternative for such Euro-rejects.

THE PROBLEM OF EUROPE

The apparently irresistible momentum of European integration is not,
however, without its complications and uncertainties. The levels of convergence that have been achieved throughout the European Community
are qualified by the persistence of considerable diversity of economic
structure and performance, and of culture and political perspective. Many
of the issues that require decision before full integration remain highly
contentious. Britain, under its Conservative government, proved antagonistic towards the proposed Social Chapter of the Maastricht Treaty with its
provisions, in part, for work-place rights and responsibilities (*The Economist*
1991e). Fundamental issues of sovereignty are also involved in progress
beyond the Single European Act to further levels of economic and
monetary union, especially proposals for a common currency; the

enhancement of the role and powers of the European Parliament; and the possibilities of Community control of foreign policy and the creation of a common defence force.

The persistence of substantial diversity and doubt thus bathes the European Community in a mottled light. The expectations of participating policy-makers, the aspirations of interested business enterprises, the hopes of Euro-enthusiasts and the undoubted idealism of many cooperatively inclined European citizens contrasts markedly with the persisting Euro-scepticism, if not outright hostility, of a significant number of ordinary people in a number of EC member states and the marked reluctance of their governments to accede to new levels of formal integration or to implement past agreements or Commission determinations, with rigour and regularity. Fears, too, of effective German domination of the Community might prompt growing apprehensions amongst the policy-makers and populations of other member states.

The stimulation of atavistic nationalistic impulses remains firmly within the realm of political choice and political leadership. The success of such political programmes may be considerably assisted, however, by suitable conditions, particularly significant and uncomfortable levels of unemployment. The serious levels to which unemployment has risen throughout the European Community, as illustrated by Table 6.1, clearly provides the backdrop to rising right-wing radicalism. On the other side, it also reinforces the EC's dispositions towards the preservation and promotion of Europe's economy and industry.

Table 6.1 Unemployment rates (per cent)

	EEC	USA	Japan
1975	2.9	8.5	1.9
1981	7.8	7.6	2.2
1985	10.6	7.2	2.6
1986	10.7	7.0	2.8

Source: Europe in Figures (1987), Luxembourg: Statistical Office of the European Communities.

Persisting variation in economic structure and performance underlies the differing impact of the EC, and its central programmes, upon member states. The Common Agricultural Policy (CAP), by subsidising small-scale agricultural producers and taxing substantial importers of agricultural products, had a highly unequal impact throughout the EC, particularly during the first decade of Britain's membership. Indeed, it was only after prolonged and acrimonious negotiations that Britain was able to secure a significant reduction in the massive financial transfers to other EC states, generated by the CAP, the common external tariff and, more latterly, value added tax (VAT) receipts. However, the impact of reforms, rebate and regional assistance remains limited, with the persistence of massive imbalances in the net financial benefits and burdens of member states. In 1987, after major changes had been implemented, the distribution of costs and advantages ranged from net receipts from the EC of 1536.5 million and 389.6 million ECUs by Greece and Portugal respectively and net payments to the EC of 4842.8 million and 2606 million ECUs by West Germany and the United Kingdom respectively (Shackleton 1990: 66). Such disparities of advantages and disadvantages reinforce the difficulties engendered by the experience of substantial variations in member states' balances of trade with one another, as indicated subsequently in this discussion.

Such economic differences can, however, be reduced and their more serious consequences compensated, by appropriate Community policies: industrial and regional. The EC's Regional Policies, orchestrated through the European Coal and Steel Community (ECSC), the European Agricultural Guidance and Guarantee Fund (EAGGF); the European Investment Bank (EIB); the European Social Fund (ESF); and the European Regional Development Fund (ERDF), allow support for specific regions within the member states and, where warranted, for the member states themselves (Harrop 1989: ch. 6). An increase in disbursements of such structural funding has been seen as one possible vehicle for partially reimbursing Britain for her considerable financial contribution to the Community. EC members with lower levels of industrialisation and GDP per capita are also being provided with considerable levels of assistance through these policy instruments; estimated at 5 per cent of GDP for Greece, Portugal and the Irish Republic and 1.5 per cent of that of Spain (Pinder 1991: 158).

With uneven development a persistent tendency within the modern international political economy, sustained policies to redistribute wealth and prosperity substantially may be necessary but will remain controversial and fragile politically. The resentments of those from whom resources are being withdrawn will never be far from the surface, as the reaction against US welfare policies during Reagan's Presidency indicated. Success for the EC's cohesion programme will therefore require a combination of moral leadership, and skilful policy formation and implementation if corrosive reactions are to be pre-empted. The persistence of a 'democratic deficit', or the insensitive imposition of 'majority' decisions on reluctant member states, might damage the EC's prospects for avoiding difficult distributional disputes.

Substantial politico-economic divergences within its membership will, however, create continuing problems for the development and implementation of EC policy in the future. The vitality of different states and regions, and their responsiveness to various policy initiatives, will also remain major complications. So, too, will serious variations in capacities for, and dispositions towards, the implementation of the EC's rules and regulations. Chronic disregard of the spirit and letter of major Community treaties and agreements, and neglect of the Commission's regulations, directives and decisions, weakens the practical impact of EC policies. Moreover, such national delinquency is corrosive of the spirit of the EC and destructive of the commitment of its more conscientious members.

The disillusionment of the law-abiding members of the EC may prove particularly troublesome as further steps towards economic and political unification are considered. The elimination of effective state customs and immigration borders will render all EC members vulnerable to the inadvertent importation of substandard products and the unrestrained movement of unauthorised entrants. The anxieties of member states will be all the greater if the EC's less resolute members prove open to a continuing wave of migration from the southern shores of the Mediterranean or mass movements of population from central and eastern Europe.

Whether the European Community will continue to widen and deepen its membership is, however, a complex issue. A number of contrasting perspectives upon European integration seek to answer this question: perspectives which differ in their identification of fundamental forces and mechanisms in human affairs and in their prognoses for the future of the European project.

DOCTRINES AND DYNAMICS OF EUROPEAN INTEGRATION

The debate between 'federalists' and 'functionalists' (and latterly neo-functionalists) dominated early discussion of European integration.[3] Neo-mercantilists and radical sceptics soon, however, contributed their additional views and insights. Sharing a common commitment to integration, federalists have emphasised the role of prior political commitment (Pinder 1991: 213), while functionalists/neo-functionalists have looked towards 'spill over' from areas of intensifying economic interaction to prompt ever closer political ties (George 1990: ch. 2).

For both schools of thought, closer economic and political association promises greater harmony amongst peoples. Federalists remain, at heart, political voluntarists, while functionalists/neo-functionalists maintain the optimistic beliefs of nineteenth-century liberals in the general benefits of free international trade and the pacifying effects of growing levels of economic interdependence amongst societies.[4] The promotion of economic integration is thus a political imperative within the logic of neo-functionalism.

Neo-mercantilist views of European integration reflect doubts about the automatic benefits of *laissez-faire* economic systems. Moreover, states are seen to have a wide range of political and military responsibilities and purposes, for which a wide variety of means, including measures of economic and industrial direction and control, may properly be employed (Jones 1986, 1988; George 1990b). Indeed, states have often been seen to play a central part in economic developments, often for military purposes (Howard 1976) and thereby promoted industrial society (Hall 1985: Part 1). Structuralist and 'post-Sraffian' arguments reinforce these views that governments, national or supranational, can play a decisive role in the promotion and preservation of the general economic and industrial strength and well-being of societies.[5]

The EC's promotion of regional economic and industrial strength is thus welcomed by neo-mercantilists. Particular favour is bestowed upon a range of specific programmes, including the Joint European Taurus (JET) nuclear fusion project and the European Research Co-ordination Agency (EUREKA), which are directed at the development of Europe's performance in training, technology, and information processing and communication.

Policies to influence the structure of industry are also welcomed. The Coal and Steel Community and efforts to reduce the European steel industry to viable dimensions have continued into the 1980s (Barnes with Preston 1988: 94–7) Competition has also been promoted where appropriate, with the EC's Commission becoming increasingly active in the monitoring of mergers and takeovers. The relationship between business and the Community is, however, complex and at times ambivalent. In some views, the EC is overwhelmingly a defensive response by European industry, seeking to create an unified region within which to enjoy economies of scale in their production, mutually beneficial alliances with other European enterprises and, possibly, a common economic barrier behind which to shelter from intensifying international competition.

However, the Commission's interference with many mergers and take-overs within industries discords, somewhat, with the views of those who see integration as the creation, and creature, of dominant, and increasingly transnational, capitalist interests (Holland 1980).

Unresolved tensions persist between the EC and its member states over industrial policy, however. Financial restriction is imposed by national governments which, with substantial domestic research and development programmes of their own, are still reluctant to see duplication at, or competition from, the European level. The EC's overall contribution to R&D within the Community thus remains relatively small in size and impact; consuming only 2.5 per cent of the Community's overall budget in the early 1980s and amounting to a mere 2 per cent of total R&D expenditure within the Community (Harrop 1989: 98).

Integration within Europe may thus have a politically integrative complexion internally, but presents a determinedly competitive face to the wider world economy: the preservation of competitiveness in areas, like chemicals, in which Europe retains a dominant global position, is to be complemented, where possible, by restored industrial vitality. For such potentialities to be realised, however, a number of persisting areas of difficulty have to be confronted and overcome by the developing European Community.

EUROPE: INTEGRATION, DISINTEGRATION AND REGIONALISM

Deep economic disparities exist within the Community. Levels of wealth vary considerably, as indicated by Table 6.2. While agriculture, forestry and fishing contributed 16.2 per cent of Greece's GDP in 1987, it was the source of only 1.8 per cent of the Federal Republic of Germany's GDP. Again, the contribution of 18.8 per cent of Greece's GDP by manufacturing, contrasted sharply with the 30.5 per cent of Federal Germany's GDP derived from manufacturing industry (Office for Official Publications of the European Communities 1990: 20). The patterns of trade amongst the EC member states are also highly imbalanced, as Table 6.3 indicates, with Germany's 1987 intra-EC balance of payments surplus of 26,211 million ECU contrasting with the French and British deficits of 14,691 and 12,970 million ECU respectively.

The size and control of the EC's budget also divides those of contending views of Europe's future. The EC's annual budget was slightly less than 1 per cent of the GNP of the EC by the mid-1980s (up from some 0.5 per cent in 1975), amounting to a mere 2.8 per cent of the member states'

Table 6.2   GNP per capita in the EC, 1989 (US dollars)

Portugal	4,250
Greece	5,350
Eire	8,710
Spain	9,330
United Kingdom	14,610
Italy	15,120
Netherlands	15,920
Belgium	16,220
France	17,820
West Germany	20,440
Denmark	20,450
Luxembourg	N/A

Source: World Bank (1991) *World Development Report, 1991*, Oxford: Oxford University Press, table 1, pp. 104–5.

Table 6.3   Intra-EC balances of trade, 1985, 1986 and 1987 (millions of ECU)

	1985	1986	1987	1988	1989	1990
Belgium–Luxembourg	−1,430	1,931	952	5,693	6,988	5,400
Denmark	−2,087	−2,208	−1,034	−265	208	894
West Germany	9,477	20,256	26,211	31,338	34,724	23,452
Greece	−3,109	−3,076	−3,080	−2,175	−4,037	−5,308
Spain	2,626	−635	−3,192	−5,326	−9,231	−9,987
France	−15,334	−13,969	−14,691	−15,696	−18,909	−17,744
Ireland	−57	570	1,753	2,221	2,493	2,232
Italy	−6,433	−3,347	−4,790	−5,350	−7,393	−5,170
Netherlands	19,924	15,456	12,352	17,738	23,804	28,044
Portugal	−18	−667	−1,747	−3,470	−3,249	−3,815
United Kingdom	−3,617	−12,676	−12,970	−24,208	−25,435	−18,084

Source: *External Trade Monthly Statistics European Communities*, Statistical Office of the European Communities, 1988, no. 12, p. 37; and *External Trade Monthly Statistics European Communities*, Statistical Office of the European Communities, 1992, no. 1, table 6, pp. 24–9.

governmental budgets. This could, however, expand if the increase of the EC's share of value added taxes collected within its member countries, from the 1.4 per cent maximum agreed in 1984, to the 1.6 per cent suggested at the 1988 EC Summit, was to be accepted (Harrop 1989: 155).

The concession of a modest 14 per cent increase in the budget between 1988 and 1992, and the introduction of a new tax on the difference between member states' GNPs and VAT bases – the 'fourth financial' resource – signalled continuing pressures for an expansion of EC expenditures (Pinder 1991: 60).

While the primary focus of this discussion rests upon economic issues, such issues do not stand alone within the complex processes of European development and integration. A major issue, therefore, is the match between political developments within Europe and economic changes. Any substantial mismatches between the 'political' and the 'economic' carry dangers ranging from serious obstacles to continued progress, through to the collapse of the entire integration project. Developments in human affairs are, moreover, rarely smooth, linear and readily reversible. Failure to progress might well expose Europe to a highly uncertain future.

There are two areas of potential mismatch between political and economic developments within contemporary Europe. Many contemporary observers and participants are concerned about uneven institutional developments within the EC and the wider Europe. This general concern subsumes two more specific, but ultimately interrelated, issues: the development of political and managerial institutions sufficient to cope with the requirements generated by the further advance of economic and monetary integration within the European Community; and, of no less moment, the establishment of a better balance between the various 'political' institutions of the EC – the Commission, the Council of Ministers and, most pertinently, the European Parliament.

Considerations of each set of issues are much complicated by their connections with persisting differences about the ultimate level and extent of integration within the European Community and associated issues of sovereignty. Concerns about the character of a European Central Bank are thus acute only for those who believe in the desirability, even necessity, of a common currency for the EC. In contrast, the 'democratic deficit'[6] that many claim to identify in the imbalance between the considerable 'powers' of the Commission and the Council of Ministers on the one side and the relative weakness of the European Parliament on the other, is of little concern to those who believe that national governments express the real democratic sentiments and requirements of their peoples. Such diversities of approach do not, however, preclude unintended institutional inconsistencies and incongruities that could prove difficult to remedy.

There are also persisting dangers of mismatches between institutional developments, on the one hand, and popular political sentiments, on the other. The momentum developed by a potent mix of enthusiastic participants and the 'logic of events' carries a continuing threat of institutional developments that outpace the expectations, aspirations and, ultimately, the acceptance of significant proportions of the populations of some member states. Indeed, the very psycho-political remoteness of Brussels, and other EC institutions, might further reinforce many of the 'nationalisms' now resurfacing throughout the EC and its neighbouring states. The dangers lie not so much with the grand steps towards integration and institutional innovation at the highest level of Community affairs, but in the effects of specific policies and measures which are found to be costly at the local level. Where sentiments of Community-wide benefit are lacking, locally costly initiatives may prove unacceptable and, hence, politically explosive. Carrying populations along with Community-wide institutional developments and policy innovations will thus continue to confront European integrationists with some of their most pressing tasks, the neglect of which could endow Europe with horizontal fracture lines, to complicate its persisting vertical lines of friction.

The complex relationship between institutional developments and popular political sentiments thus demonstrates the role of political debate, argument and leadership in generating acceptance for the principles, and ultimately the practices, of political life. Differing views on how Europe, and its constituent peoples, should best be organised and further developed, persist. The future will be determined by the persuasive abilities of those who seek to impress their various constituencies: local, 'national' and European.

STATE DISSOLUTION AND A EUROPE OF REGIONS

The future of Europe turns around the unresolved counter-claims of European identity, nation-states, and subnational regions and, in some cases trans-border, peoples. Such contending affiliations complicate the otherwise simple division between strong federalists and weak confederalists. Figure 6.1 captures some, but not all, of the identifiable positions on Europe's future.

Many of the differences on Europe's future are sharp. Euro-federalists see a strong, unified EC as the best means of suppressing the worst manifestations of nationalism and promoting European economic mobilisation. Conservative statists believe that the established states of Europe alone are capable of giving sound and stable expression to currents of national sentiment that continue to flow throughout modern Europe and that states can still furnish much of the framework for successful economic development, given some Community support and assistance in appropri-

	Federal	Confederal
Strong central government(s)	**Euro-federalists**	**Conservative statists**
	pro-Commission	pro-Council
Weak central government(s) + local powers	**Federal regionalists**	Local and Regional advocates
	pro-Parliament	**Regional Euro-minimalists**

Figure 6.1   Contrasting dispositions towards European developments

ate areas. Federal regionalists argue, in contrast, that much can be achieved through vigorous Community level actions and institutions, but only when the aspirations of a wide range of smaller national groupings and regional communities have been satisfied, possibly at the expense of established states. Regional Euro-minimalists also look to the satisfaction of national and regional wishes but remain wary of surrendering any newly won powers to an enhanced Community and its institutions.

The doctrine of 'subsidiarity' has been the rallying cry of conservative statists in their efforts to withhold power and authority from EC levels of governance in as many areas as possible and retain competence for national governments. However, the notion of subsidiarity may prove a double-edged weapon: an argument of equal potence for those who seek enhanced control and influence for the Community's regions and localities.

The size and source of the EC budget is not the only issue to stimulate division within the Community, however. The control of the budget is also a central issue, with many Euro-enthusiasts proposing an increased role for the European Parliament in the determination and scrutiny of Community spending programmes. Euro-minimalists, in contrast, continue to emphasise the role of the representatives of national governments – the Council of Ministers and the European Council, rather than the Parliament, in authorising and checking EC expenditures.

There will be a persisting tension between the harmonising and centralising tendencies of Brussels and the growing wish for local competence and self-control within many of Europe's regions and localities. The attractions of simple and coherent policy-making may run counter to the implementational advantages of policy determined through more participatory procedures and institutions. Moreover, fatal tensions might arise if the counter claims of the local, 'national' and European levels of politics remain unresolved. However, some signs of an increased responsiveness to the sensitivities of Europe's regions and localities were evidenced by the inclusion in the draft treaty on political union for the Maastricht Summit, of provisions for committees of representatives from the Community's regions and local authorities, to advise on the regional impact of EC policies; a departure which reflects the growing emphasis upon regions recently exhibited within France (*The Economist* 1991h).

Monetary integration

The intense debates over the possibility of European monetary union, with a common currency and a managerial institution, embrace all levels of possible argument: whether a common currency is intrinsically desirable; what institutional arrangements should be made for its regulation; how should such a regulatory body relate to other institutions of the European Community; and, finally, but of no less significance, how might practical, and politically acceptable, progress towards the introduction of a common currency best be orchestrated?

A common European currency would bear both advantages and disadvantages. Individuals and firms would benefit from reduced transaction costs and minimised currency risks: risks that have been made all the greater by the massive growth of internationally mobile funds during recent decades. European currency unification would, however, constrain states and their peoples in general. The utility of many traditional instruments of national economic policy would be severely reduced, including interest rates and public sector borrowing to stimulate economic recovery and growth. Moreover, a common currency would render national economies even more open and increase their exposure to effects generated elsewhere within the Community. Thus, increases in interest rates within Germany, for example, would exert even stronger upward pressures upon British interest rates, if Britain returned to the European exchange rate mechanism (*The Guardian* 1991a).

The maintenance of national currencies is thus a more complex matter than the preservation of a mere symbol of national sovereignty. The conditions under which a common currency might be introduced are also critical. Clear rules have been prescribed for the establishment of a European currency. A limitation of official interest rates to no more than 2 per cent above the average levels of the three best performing member states will be required. Taxation policies within the EC may also have to move together over time. Cumulative national debt will be restricted to a maximum of 60 per cent of the respective member state's gross domestic product (GDP). The public sector borrowing requirements of 'national' governments (the difference between government receipts from taxation, etc., and its annual expenditure) will also be limited to a maximum 3 per cent of GDP in any year; with consequential constraints on governmental support for economic and industrial expansion.

Given the mixed record of the European monetary system's exchange rate mechanism, since its inception in 1978, it is unsurprising that there are seriously divergent views about the nature and pace of future monetary integration. The matrix of contrasting positions on a common currency, in Figure 6.2, illustrates this diversity.

Obligatory Common Currency + Independent Central Bank	'Voluntary' Common Currency + Independent Central Bank
Obligatory Common Currency + Central Bank Controlled by Council of Ministers	'Voluntary' Common Currency + Central Bank Controlled by Council of Ministers

Figure 6.2   Contending approaches to the common currency and a central bank

Britain's position in the period preceding the Maastricht Summit of December 1991 was for a common currency, which hesitant states, like Britain, would not be obliged to accept initially, and for a European central bank, that would remain under the political authority of the Council of Ministers. In contrast, Germany proposed the comprehensive adoption of the common currency from the time of its ultimate introduction, after a three-stage preparatory process (1991–4; 1994–7 and post-1997), and its regulation by a politically independent European central bank. The acceptance of a final, fall-back date of 1999 for the adoption of a common currency if at all possible, marked merely a minor compromise in the German position. Contrasting positions of such sharpness fully reflect, and will inevitably continue to demonstrate, divergent expectations and aspirations respecting all aspects of the future integration of Europe, financial, economic, political and security.

Europe's defence industries in a new international order

Defence, military production and defence procurement are not merely matters of security interest for the states of the developing EC. Defence industries continue to form a significant part of the economies of many European states; and a vital part of those of Great Britain and France. For much of the post-war era, more than 50 per cent of Britain's officially funded research and development was devoted to defence purposes.[7] In France, more than 330,000 jobs may be directly involved in, and more than 700,000 indirectly dependent upon, military research, production and procurement (*The Economist* 1984). Significant proportions of industrial output in Germany, Italy and Belgium are also military in character.

The recent growth of interest in a new security framework for Europe (see Chapter 5) reflects both concerns about the long-term commitment of the United States of America and aspirations to deepen the level of political integration within the EC. However, concerns about the health of the European defence industry, and the broader industrial sectors within which it is located, remain close to the surface. Thus, in 1987, 62.6 per cent of the output of the European aerospace industry, which employed some 489,000 people in 1988, was military (Office for Official Publications of the European Communities 1990: 13–35). A developing pan-EC defence and security structure, possibly through an enhanced and enlarged Western European Union (WEU), would encourage further standardisation of military equipment throughout western Europe and promote the prospects of its local suppliers, when operating singly or in the consortia that have emerged within Europe's aerospace sector.

Thus far, an intimate symbiosis of arms manufacturers, military establishments and state bureaucracies has characterised armaments' procurement and export efforts at a state level within Europe. A common European defence structure might sit happily with a more integrated Europe-wide system of armaments' production and export. The effects of such developments upon Europe's relations with the USA and the Third World might, however, prove complex and potentially problematical.

The development of a new European security structure thus has potential implications for the promotion of some of Europe's high technology industries. However, the need for such a European security initiative reflects, in part at least, a concern that growing trans-Atlantic trade rivalries might eventually reduce the USA's commitment to the defence of western Europe. Interest in a European security arrangement is further reinforced by a combination of a general wish to express the growing economic strength of an integrated Europe in political and military terms, with a more specific concern to develop a capacity to deal with the political and economic dangers emanating from an increasingly fragmented central and eastern Europe. The future of European security thus captures the political-military-industrial complex of issues and interests in a profound, albeit complex, manner.

EUROPE AND THE WIDER WORLD

Europe's future development will thus both influence and be influenced by developments in a number of aspects of the wider international political economy, including the growing role of transnational corporations (TNCs); and the condition and prospects of the developing world. The CAP continues to colour relations with the developing world and world trade negotiations under the General Agreement on Tariffs and Trade (GATT).

Transnational corporations (TNCs) and the imperative for integration

The EC constitutes a potent response to the paradox of contemporary state sovereignty, created by the nature and functioning of TNCs. As states have sought, jealously, to preserve their individual sovereignties, so they have perpetuated a politically and legally fragmented international landscape across which TNCs have been free to roam. As fragmented sovereignties have endowed TNCs with unique opportunities for manoeuvre and manipulation, so the effective sovereignty of states in some areas of critical importance has been compromised, if not fatally damaged.

Such limitations upon state capabilities have been exemplified by the TNCs' ability to undertake transfer pricing, thereby minimising tax payments, evading a range of national economic regulations, and orchestrating a rapid and substantial international movement of funds (Murray 1981). TNCs have also been able to exploit 'dowry chasing' opportunities offered by national and regional authorities, seeking to attract inward investment and have, moreover, often proved to be swift to depart once financial incentives come to an end (*The Guardian* 1984).

The combined effects of such TNC capabilities and opportunities has been to reduce the effectiveness of many traditional instruments of national economic and industrial policy, thereby stimulating proposals for their control and regulation. While the individual state may be cautious towards TNCs, unilateral control and regulation may prove ineffectual, and even self-defeating, for all but the strongest and wealthiest of national economies. The EC offers a regional answer to the problems of disunity and 'free riding' (Olson 1965; Frohlich and Oppenheimer 1978) that have characteristically undermined attempts to orchestrate effective global co-operation in all substantive areas.

The adoption of firm policies has, however, been constrained by the spread of the EC's own TNCs, the persistence of ideological diversity amongst the governments of member states, and perceptions that inward investment into Community countries offers a 'solution' to the many problems of unemployment, low investment, faltering research and development and declining industrial competitiveness (Barry Jones 1985). However, policies on competition, mergers and takeovers, official procurement, research and development funding and limits on 'imported' goods have been deployed in the EC's efforts to regulate TNCs.

Despite some academic doubts (Thomsen and Nicolaides 1991), EC members have also voiced suspicions that many new ventures or acquisitions by non-EC TNCs are essentially a device for preserving market access within the Community in the face of additional curbs on imports that might be erected in the future. Thus, the EC has sought to designate the vehicles built by Japanese subsidiaries in Great Britain as part of the overall market share allocated to those companies under the 'voluntary' export agreements concluded between the EC and Japanese car exporters (*The Economist* 1991b).

Europe and the developing world

The EC's continuing relationship with the developing world has been mixed in its sources and consequences. The Yaounde Convention of 1967 and the Lomé Agreements, I, II, III and IV, for the periods 1975–9, 1979–85, 1985–90 and 1990–95, confirmed preferential access to EC markets for a group of former colonies gathered together under the title of African, Caribbean and Pacific group (ACP). The Lomé Agreements also introduced the STABEX and SYSMIN schemes to stabilise ACP revenues from exports of primary products and minerals; and provided increasing sums of financial assistance; 3.5 billion, 5.5 billion, 8.5 billion and 12 billion ECUs respectively.

The advantages secured by the ACP states from their association with the EC have been achieved, in part, at the expense of those other developing countries that have been denied similar preferential arrangements. Moreover, the EC's preservation of the CAP, and operation of the Multi-Fibre Arrangement, has continued to distort substantial portions of its trade with the ACP countries. Finally, the benefits of the apparently generous EC Generalised System of Preferences has been largely confined to a few exporters of machinery and electrical goods (Weston *et al.* 1980: 158).

Overall, the EC's relations with the ACP states have been criticised as a form of neo-imperialism. Moreover, the benefits that the ACP do secure from association with the EC may not prove robust, as the attention of the Community members turns increasingly towards internal concerns and the demands of their eastern neighbours.

The Common Agricultural Policy

The Common Agricultural Policy (CAP) is considered last in this discussion of the European economic agenda for its past, present and future development are pivotal for the wider European agenda and central to an interpretation of the nature and potentialities of the developing European Community. Nothing has thrown the mercantilist complexion of the EC into sharper focus than the CAP and its defence in the face of persisting international criticism, pressure and agitated negotiations within the Uruguay Round of GATT.

The CAP was an integral part of the Treaty of Rome. The primary aims were to employ price support mechanisms to ensure secure agricultural supplies, maintain reasonable standards of living for the community of agricultural producers, increase agricultural productivity, provide consumers with food stuffs at reasonable prices and ensure general stability in agricultural markets. Unfortunately, growing surpluses of agricultural produce were one of the more visible results of maintaining high, guaranteed prices for output, as farmers were encouraged to produce ever more and consumers were discouraged from increasing consumption by the higher prices resulting from price-maintaining intervention in the market.

The consequences of the CAP have been profound. Growing surpluses of many agricultural products were generated and reduced only by subsidised exports onto the world market, with destabilising effects on world prices and the earnings of other producers, some of whom were poor developing countries. With EC agricultural exports increasing by some 300 per cent between 1973 and 1986, world prices for wheat, meat and sugar were estimated to have been reduced by between 9 and 17 per cent (Barnes and Preston 1988: 115).

Within the EC itself, the CAP has also been responsible for significant flows of income between member states and between urban and rural communities: estimated at some 2.3 per cent of national income between 1978 and 1983 (Van Den Noort in Coffey 1988: 31–51). Britain's net contribution of £1165 billion in 1980 was largely a result of the CAP, while higher food prices have contributed to the inflationary pressures experienced by states like the United Kingdom.

While measures to tame the CAP have been introduced by the EC, it remains so central to the Community that it became a major stumbling block to the completion of the Uruguay Round of talks under GATT, with total collapse being avoided only by a reduction of the demands made upon the EC for major reductions in its financial support for agriculture (*The Economist* 1991g).

CONCLUSIONS: HAZARDOUS JOURNEYS AND UNCERTAIN FUTURES

No realistic analysis of the complex issues surrounding the development of Europe, as it approaches the twenty-first century, can afford to treat politics and economics separately from one another. Europe is embarked upon a journey into an uncertain economic future; a vital influence upon which will be the character, cohesiveness and capabilities of its political institutions. Unless a cohesive political outlook is developed throughout the EC, and policies are constructed with considerable sensitivity, the willingness to accept European policies will be lacking amongst those who bear their costs. The need for such sentiments will become all the greater as continued economic and monetary union restricts the abilities of member states to direct their affairs unilaterally, leaving them increasingly dependent upon Community policies and programmes for relief and recompense. Regional and redistributive issues will thus be at the heart of Europe's future political economy.

The course of Europe's economic path will be a product of the interaction of three powerful vectors: the further development of the EC; the economic development or disintegration of the states of central and eastern Europe (including the nearer successor states of the Soviet Union); and the general shaping of the global political economy. The concerns that underlie many of the specific issues surveyed above will influence the direction assumed by the EC and the wider world economy. Developments within each area of concern will, equally, provide early indications of the emergent patterns within the political economies of Europe and the wider world.

At the heart of the economic agenda for Europe, and most particularly the EC, are the twin problems of maintaining competitiveness externally while managing diversity and regional disparities internally. The ultra-liberal approach to these problems would be to combine vigorous deregulation, and the freeing of market forces, with rapid economic harmonisation throughout the European Community. Neo-mercantilist and structuralist dispositions would take the Community and its institutions further down the path of support for research and development, pro-grammes of industrial support and promotion, improved training and education and the introduction of many of the measures associated with the now highly controversial social programme.

The problems posed by the post-communist societies of central and eastern Europe will complicate Europe's future. The economic pro-gramme of the EC will emphasise aid to ease the conditions of the populations of central and eastern Europe and support for the reconstruc-tion of their economies. The eventual admission to the EC of applicants from central and eastern Europe will be possible only when their econ-omies have been substantially redeveloped and when the EC's own policies, such as the CAP, have been so modified as to make the arrival of the new members economically manageable.

Unfortunately, the growing preoccupation of Europe with its own affairs and internal developments may well reduce its concern for, and provision of resources for, the developing world. Relationships with the ACP countries are likely to continue, and to be emphasised where they involve strategically or economically sensitive issues. However, the EC's funding of aid for the ACP countries and the development of helpful policies may both suffer in the train of the new European agenda. The CAP, with its generally damaging effects upon non-EC economies, will be modified only under pressure within wider global economic negotia-tions, or in response to the internal needs of the EC, rather than by benign attitudes towards less favoured economies.

Neo-mercantilist and Economic Realist impulses within the European Community could remain relatively benign if developments in the world economy and the domestic political systems of its member states remain favourable. There are, however, two serious, and possibly interrelated, areas of danger. If competitive pressures within the global economy continue to intensify, then the impulses towards 'Fortress Europe' may also rise. Worse, the resurgence of ultra-right wing political movements within many of Europe's member states could congeal into a revival of the Euro-fascism that so disfigured the 1930s and 1940s. Insensitivity in the centres of power of the European project could accelerate and intensify such unwelcome responses. A stable and benign European future will thus require the most careful handling of politico-economic developments both external and internal to the present European Community.

NOTES

1 For a further discussion of this embryonic regionalisation see: R. Gilpin (1987) *The Political Economy of International Relations*, Princeton, NJ: Princeton University Press.

2 On which see: Barry R. J. Jones and P. Willetts (eds) (1984) *Interdependence on Trial: Studies in the Theory and Reality of Contemporary Interdependence*, London: Pinter, esp. chs. 1, 2 and 6.

3 For discussions of these doctrines see: A. J. Groom and P. Taylor (1975) *Functionalism: Theory and Practice in International Relations*, London: University of London Press, part 1.

4 For a discussion of such arguments focusing on the origins and effects of economic interdependence see: B. Buzan (1984) 'Economic structure and international security', *International Organization*, 38, 4, Autumn, 597–624.

5 For more details on such structuralist and 'post-Sraffian' ideas see: C. Edwards (1985) *The Fragmented World: Competing Perspectives on Trade, Money and Crisis*, London: Methuen, esp. chs. 2, 3 and 4.

6 On which see: S. Williams (1991) 'Sovereignty and accountability in the European Community', in R. Keohane and S. Hoffmann, (eds) *The New European Community: Decisionmaking and Institutional Change*, Boulder, Colo.: Westview Press, pp. 155–176.

7 See K. Pavitt (1981) 'Technology in British industry: a suitable case for improvement', in C. Carter, (ed.), *Industrial Policy and Innovation*, London, Heinemann, table 7.6, p. 104.

Chapter 7

The environment agenda
Joanna Spear

INTRODUCTION

Environmental issues have achieved a new prominence since the end of
the Cold War and are a key element of the European agenda for the
twenty-first century. However, the types of environmental issues considered of greatest importance are different for eastern and western Europe
and there are also contrasting traditions and priorities among western states.
In the former communist states of eastern Europe environmentalists played
a key role in undermining the authority of the communist rulers. Subsequently economic development has become the first priority resulting in
environmental issues being discussed mainly in terms of cleaning up
polluted areas. Consequently, since 1989 the role of environmental groups
has diminished and they once again find themselves in opposition.

The states of western Europe differ as to the aspects of the environment
considered most important. For example, in the Scandinavian countries
and (West) Germany debates have centred around nuclear power. In
Britain, the emphasis has been on preserving the countryside (as opposed
to the wilderness as in the Scandinavian countries). But throughout western
Europe environmentalism has gone beyond a parochial focus on regional
problems and solutions towards a wider-ranging debate about global
environmental issues. The same dilemma about the tension between
economic growth and environmentalism exists, but it is obviously much
less acute given the levels of development already achieved. Thus within
the new Europe we have a microcosm of the debates being played out
globally between North and South over the priority of development or
the environment. The difference is geography; in Europe the contrasting
approaches are advanced on the same continent.

Thus it is important to recognise from the outset that the problems
entailed in environmentalism are different in the two halves of Europe.
Another consequence is that common ground on environmental issues

tends to be at the lowest level; little more than pollution control, and even then there are disputes regarding the best methods to tackle problems, through voluntary action or through legislation.

Given the constraints of space it is impossible to deal with all the environmental issues emerging in Europe. Rather, the chapter will focus on those that point up wider issues and conflicts and are illustrative of key aspects of the environmental debate. In the first section of this chapter environmental activity at four different levels is examined: the global level; the system level; the state level; and the individual (substate) level. These categories show the different motors for change which operate in the area of the environment. The remainder of the chapter deals with three key aspects of environmentalism: environmental diplomacy; the relationship between the environment and development; and environmental security.

ENVIRONMENTAL ISSUES AT THE GLOBAL LEVEL

At the global level there are several different environmental initiatives. This section focuses on the work of the United Nations, other international organisations, and the Group of Seven (G7 – seven leading industrial powers).

The first global initiative on environmental issues came in 1972 with the establishment of the United Nations Environmental Programme (UNEP). The aim was to establish the means for increasing the attention paid to environmental issues (Dahlberg *et al.* 1985: 57–67). The original focus of the agency was on conservation, preservation and restoration (Holdgate *et al.* 1982). During the 1980s, however, the focus of UNEP and the international community came to rest more on issues involving prevention. This is reflected in the range of issues discussed at the Earth Summit and the resulting UN document Agenda 21. Agenda 21 is the United Nation's forty-chapter plan for cleaning up the environment and introducing sustainable development. Although the document is not legally binding, it is designed to force the pace of change on environmental issues (Vidal 1992c). As demonstrated at the 1992 United Nations Conference on the Environment and Development (UNCED, commonly known as the Earth Summit) held in Rio de Janeiro, Brazil, UNEP's international status is increasing. This increased status is not matched within the United Nations structure as UNEP is not currently categorised as a specialised agency. Discussions are currently underway concerning raising UNEP's profile (Plant 1992: 135).

The United Nations Conference on the Law of the Sea (UNCLOS), convened by the General Assembly in 1973 has important implications for future global environmental negotiations as it was the first to accept the notion of certain resources as a 'common heritage of mankind' and worked on the basis that the sea should be managed for the benefit of all and belong to none. After nine years of negotiation the draft convention was completed in 1982 and has been approved by over 140 countries.

Several international organisations deal with environmental issues as an adjunct to their major functions. For example, the Food and Agriculture Organisation (FAO) which deals with food production, seed types, fertilisers, etc. inevitably confronts environmental issues. The same is true for the World Bank and the International Monetary Fund (IMF) through their work on development (see below). The dispute that has plagued the Uruguay Round of the General Agreement on Tariffs and Trade (GATT) has an environmental dimension. According to a World Commission on the Environment and Development Report of 1987, agricultural subsidies and trade barriers in developed countries have encouraged the over-use of soils and chemicals, the pollution of both water resources and foods with these chemicals, and the degradation of the countryside (OECD 1989: 16–17). However, it should be noted that this approach, advanced by free marketeers, is contested by those who argue that an unrestrained market leads to greater environmental damage.

The Group of Seven (G7) is composed of the heads of the major industrialised states and is a powerful forum for discussion of the management of the international economy. Only latterly has the G7 given any attention to environmental issues, first addressing them at its July 1989 meeting by stating that there should be an urgent international effort to understand and guard the earth's ecological balance. This call was repeated at subsequent annual meetings, but as yet the G7 has not moved beyond rhetoric towards any coordinated action (Rowlands 1992: 30).

Global activity on environmental issues is therefore quite patchy and only partially coordinated. The role of UNEP is weakened because of its low status in the UN system and its relatively small budget. Environmental issues also bring into play several international organisations whose *raison d'etre* seems to conflict with the aims of environmentalists; for example, the primary interests of the G7, World Bank and IMF are in promoting economic growth.

ENVIRONMENTAL ISSUES AT THE SYSTEM LEVEL

The European Community (EC) is the only international organisation with the power to agree environmental policies which are binding on its member states. As McCormick has noted 'No organization anywhere has yet achieved anything approaching the level of change promoted by the EC' (McCormick 1991: 128), yet the environmental issue was taken on only latterly by the Community. The issue was first addressed in the 1973 Programme of Action, and additional programmes were agreed in 1977, 1982 and 1987. However, it was not until 1986 with the passing of the Single European Act that environmental policy was given constitutional status. Article 25 of the Act said that the Community would take action on the environment when objectives could be better achieved by working at the Community level.

The move to a Single European Market has important implications for environmental issues (Geddes 1988: 826). Following the failure of the Danish electorate to ratify the Maastricht Treaty there has been much discussion of the future of the 1992 Single European Market project – and additionally over the Community's role in environmental legislation. It is not currently clear how much environmental legislation will be handled at Community level, for in the aftermath of the Danish referendum, there is talk of the environment being one of the areas being turned back to the individual states under the doctrine of subsidiarity (Palmer 1992a). In a sense, this is proof of the success of the EC on environmental matters. The stated desire of the British to see this issue become subject to subsidiarity is a way of flagging that they wish the EC to slow down on environmental policy.

One of the first agreements achieved by the EC was a 1987 Large Combustion Plant (LCP) Directive to limit acid emissions. This Directive was the subject of five years of intensive and acrimonious negotiations and contains a complex formula for reduction deadlines and three target dates (Grubb 1990: 72). The fact that the most environmentally advanced system level organisation, with a relatively homogeneous membership, went through such a traumatic negotiation does not augur well for global negotiations on reducing acid emissions.

The EC is currently negotiating the introduction of a carbon tax on industry intended to reduce carbon dioxide emissions to 1990 levels by the year 2000. The idea was first mooted in 1989 (Plant 1992: 127). The tax would increase the cost of oil by $US3 a barrel and is intended to spur industry into more efficient production and energy conservation. It has been calculated that the tax would lead to a drop in growth of between 0.04 and 0.2 per cent per year (Gardner 1991/92). The tax is an unusual move as the European Commission has decided to act although there is still no clear scientific consensus as to the scale of the threat. The EC has thus adopted a 'no regrets' policy on curbing carbon emissions because of the other benefits the tax will bring, for example, energy conservation (Lascelles 1992).

The tax has been opposed within the EC by a coalition of European industries and several governments. They have lobbied against the tax on the basis that it would threaten the EC's global competitiveness (Palmer 1992). This is actually taken into account in the tax as energy intensive industries such as chemicals, steel, cement and paper are all exempt from it. There would also be economic help for those industries for whom implementation was financially difficult. Despite these attempts to mollify opposition, industry was still opposed as the tax would be a unilateral control on EC business. The former EC Environment Minister Carlo Ripa di Meana met with Russian and Ukrainian ministers with the intention of persuading them to adopt similar measures to reduce carbon dioxide emissions. The Ministers told him flatly that the new states would not agree to meet the EC target (Vidal 1992a). Opponents of the tax seem to have blocked its progress by arguing that it should only be implemented when the USA and Japan adopt parallel controls and thus end incentives for non-participation.

At the European system level, the major environmental initiatives have emerged from the EC. This suggests that the system level is the more appropriate one for reaching international agreements. This is because a regional approach avoids many of the conflicts being played out at the global level (for example, the north–south conflict) because of the hete-rogeneity of the actors. However, as is shown below, the homogeneity of Europe on environmental issues is relative and implementation of en-vironmental directives is patchy across Europe.

ENVIRONMENTAL ISSUES AT THE STATE LEVEL

The different levels of environmentalism adopted by states are best illus-trated by using Organisation of Economic Cooperation and Development (OECD) categories. The OECD suggests that there are several generations of environmental policies. The first generation of policies are a response to pollution problems and involve reactive damage-control measures and clean-up programmes. Second-generation environmental policies concern the anticipation and prevention of environmental problems. Third-generation environmental policies, which began to emerge in the 1980s, involve environmental factors being taken into account in policy formation (OECD 1989). The environmental policies and practices of states of the former communist eastern bloc are still in the first-generation stage. These countries are more concerned with employment, housing, providing for basic needs and only recently have they begun to institute pollution clean-ups (French 1991). By contrast, environmental policies in most western European states have entered the second generation and in many states are now in the third generation. This is a reflection of levels of development and affluence; having achieved economic growth the governments and people are then able to turn to quality of life issues such as the environment.

Within Europe the levels of resources and attention devoted to environmental issues varies considerably. This is true even between the states of western Europe. Although the EC has moved a long way towards harmonising environmental standards among its members, it is still possible to differentiate between what Philip Lowe has called 'lead' and 'lag' states in Europe (McCormick 1991: 133). Among the obvious lead states are the Scandinavian nations, Germany, the Netherlands and Denmark. Among the lag states on environmental issues are Britain, Spain and Italy. Even these states have undertaken rhetorical commitments to improving the environment, but they have been slow to implement policies.

Germany has long been a lead state on environmental issues, in part spurred by the strength of its Green movement and Green Party. An illustration of how advanced its green policies are is that in 1993 legislation comes into force that requires all supermarkets to make provision for the return of all packaging from products so that the materials can be recycled.

The Netherlands is another environmental lead state. In autumn 1988 the government's Institute for Public Health and the Environment (RIVM) published a report on the state of the Dutch environment. The report looked at sixteen key environmental issues and concluded that the Dutch environment was still degrading (despite environmental changes already made). The report sent shock waves throughout the country and there were demands that the report should form the basis for a plan of action. In 1989 the first Dutch National Environmental Policy Plan was published. The plan makes the achievement of sustainable development within one generation its official goal. To achieve this, 220 actions are to be taken, covering the global, regional and domestic arenas. It is estimated that the plan will cost approximately £5 billion per annum by 1994. The plan places the Dutch at the forefront of environmental policies and is viewed as a model for other states to follow. However, within the Netherlands the plan has come under sustained attack from environmentalists who consider that the plan does not go far enough (Wams 1992). Indeed, if the plan is compared with the actions urged by the RIVM report, it falls far short of what is required to make a significant difference.

Several of the European lead states have taken unilateral actions designed to tackle global problems, even before international treaties and protocols have been agreed. For example, Finland, the Netherlands and Sweden have all introduced carbon taxes since 1990. However, none of the taxes is at a level high enough to spur major changes in energy use (Postel and Flavin 1991: 183).

Britain was not always considered a lag state on environmental issues, indeed, she was the initiator of the first generation of environmental policies, for example the path-breaking 1863 Alkali Act and 1945 Town and Country Planning legislation. With the onset of second-generation policies in the 1970s, she began to fall back and was left further behind in the early 1980s when lead states began to introduce third generation policies. For example, for a long time the British resisted pressure from central Europe and Scandinavia to cut the level of emissions from coal-fired power stations which resulted in acid rain in mainland Europe (Porritt and Winner 1988: 10). The Thatcher government was much slower than its European counterparts to respond to growing environmental concern in the 1980s (McCormick 1989). This was a consequence of the government's political agenda which favoured deregulation and the 'unshackling' of industry, and also a reflection of the British tradition of voluntary regulation, as opposed to state legislation and enforcement. Voluntarism allows industry to enter a dialogue with the regulatory bodies to reach mutually agreed environmental standards. For example, in response to the debate over carbon dioxide emissions, which in the EC resulted in proposals for a carbon tax, the British government introduced a voluntary code of conduct for British industry (*The Guardian* 1992). The opposition political parties were slightly quicker to pick up environmental issues (Carter 1992; 1992a). Although British Prime Minister Margaret Thatcher received a United Nations award for environmental achievement, critics charged that the British government's response to growing concerns about the environment was to adopt its rhetoric, rather than its policies.

Several east European governments had begun environmental clean-up operations during the 1980s, in part responding to pressure from environmental groups (Vavrousek *et al.* 1991). Other spurs to cleaning up the environment came from increased recognition of the costs of industrial techniques (Kramer 1983). For example, by the mid-1980s the Czechoslovakian government realised that the economic benefits of growth in industrial production were being offset by the negative social and economic costs which resulted from that additional production (ZumBrunnen 1992: 107).

Ironically though, the environmental regulations of many east European countries are more stringent than those in western Europe; the problem is that they have never been implemented. Air and water quality standards are stricter because they are set solely on the basis of a scientific determination of the levels necessary to avoid problems. Moreover, as French has pointed out, 'Unlike in the West the standards do not have to survive the vicissitudes of the political process' (French 1991: 105).

The states of eastern Europe are now beginning to battle with the environmental legacy of forty years of communist rule. Many of the pollution problems have been exacerbated by the continued employment of outdated production techniques and industrial plant from the 1950s and 1960s. Moreover, because there was no realistic system of energy pricing, there were few incentives for industry to improve efficiency and conserve fuel. This led to wasteful production techniques. The types of fuel available to the majority of eastern states are low quality soft brown coals with high ash contents which are particularly polluting (Kramer 1991).

Since the 1989 revolutions there has been a forced restructuring of the east European energy market (Kramer 1991), because of the reluctance of the former Soviet Union to continue to supply subsidised oil and gas (both cleaner than indigenous brown coals) and the United Nations trade embargo on Iraq (which eastern Europe honoured, despite the fact that it had agreed an 'oil for debt' swap with Iraq just before the invasion of Kuwait). Eastern Europe has thus far been able to avoid the worst predictions associated with the 'energy shock' of 1990–91 through a combination of luck, successful bartering and international aid (Kramer 1991). The restructuring, not yet complete, will have a profound effect on the ability of these countries to meet global emissions standards.

All of the new governments of eastern Europe have announced environmental measures. However, it appears that there are two different speeds of change being adopted. Poland and former Czechoslovakia have launched ambitious clean-up programmes aimed at improving the environmental standards of existing industries or, failing that, ensuring their closure. Hungary, Bulgaria and Romania, by contrast, are moving more slowly on environmental issues. Those countries intending to move more quickly to improve the environment are likely to encounter difficulties in that the new regulatory bodies are bureaucratically quite weak when compared with the entrenched powers of heavy industry.

At the level of the state, there are many different definitions of what environmental problems are and consequently states have focused on a variety of issues. As the OECD categorisation shows, there is a long way to go before all the states of Europe harmonise their environmental policies and practices.

ENVIRONMENTAL ISSUES AT THE LEVEL OF THE INDIVIDUAL

'Green consumerism' is an activity in which people make choices about purchases bearing in mind the environmental implications of what they buy. Elements of green consumerism include new patterns of consumption, moves to vegetarianism, recycling, ethical investments and moves to a healthier lifestyle (Elkington 1990; Porritt and Winner 1988: 190). It is a reaction against the post-war ethos that consumption was a necessary part of development (Durning 1991). In certain west European countries green consumerism has had an important impact on purchasing trends and has forced manufacturers to respond to these market pressures. Green consumerism has led manufacturers to alter the content of the goods they sell, for example, no longer using chlorofluorocarbons (CFCs) as a propellent for aerosols, the modes of production (for example, the moves away from testing cosmetics on animals in Britain) and the way in which they market their products (Cowe 1992a). This last point is crucial as many businesses have merely presented themselves differently, rather than undertaking fundamental reforms, a process referred to by environmentalists as 'greenwash'.

Green pressure groups came to prominence in both halves of Europe during the 1980s. They emerged in response to the perceived environmental crises being exposed all over the continent (Porritt and Winner 1988). Particularly in east European states, but also to a degree in the west, scientists played an important role both in establishing and publicising the nature of these environmental problems and in forming pressure groups. Importantly, in several of the communist eastern bloc countries environmentalists were the only opposition groups permitted. This meant that these groups became a focus for opposition to the communist authorities and were linked to other clandestine opposition groups such as peace campaigners. Bulgaria, former Czechoslovakia, East Germany, Hungary, Poland and Romania all had green movements before the 1989 revolutions which played a role in undermining the Communist governments (Zum-Brunnen 1992: 110). For example, in the early 1980s a biologist, Janos Vargha began a campaign against a proposed hydroelectric dam on the Danube River. This campaign snowballed and was 'instrumental in the development of effective political opposition in Hungary, which eventually undermined the Communist Party's exclusive hold on power' (French 1991: 93). Environmentalists in eastern Europe focused on the Soviet Union as the major problem; the polluter not prepared to face up to its responsibilities (Schwarz 1988; Wolf 1990; Thompson 1991). In the aftermath of the 1989 Revolutions environmental activists are no longer part of the political underground but are an important part of the political landscape (Ecoglasnost 1991). However, they are now having to fight hard to implement the strong environmental mandate implicit in those Revolutions, in the face of opposition from both politicians and public who see economic growth as the immediate priority.

Within west European states, green pressure groups are strong in the environmental 'lead' states and are growing in environmental 'lag' states. The scope of groups varies considerably from conservative groups with limited agendas interested in conservation (for example, English Heritage, the National Trust) to radical groups who favour non-violent direct action and focus on environmental issues at all levels in the system (for example, Greenpeace). Groups also spring up in response to particular issues and dissolve once they are tackled. As in east European states many environmental groups are connected to other types of new social movements, such as anti-nuclear and peace groups. This is particularly true in (West) Germany where nuclear energy is an important issue which straddles both the environment and defence.

In one sense the importance of the individual level has been increased with the formation of the EC as it has enhanced the role of pressure groups in the system generally and has thus allowed groups to push environmental issues towards the top of the Community's agenda. In this way pressure groups are a bridge between the system level and the individual. For many pressure groups within 'lag' states this is seen as a distinct advantage. However, for some pressure groups within environmental 'lead' states such as Germany, the EC is seen as putting a break on, rather than enhancing their role (McCormick 1991: 131–3).

The current position of green parties in Europe is very mixed and it is hard to establish any clear trends. Focusing on the west European states illustrates the apparently contradictory trends. In France, the traditionally weak Green Party won 14 per cent of the vote in the 1992 regional elections and are expected to perform well in the national elections. However, all opposition parties benefited at the expense of the socialist government in the regional elections, so this may also be a protest vote. In recent general elections both the Finnish and Belgian Green Parties made substantial gains, but the German and Swedish Green Parties lost all their seats as they fell below the proportional representation thresholds. Similarly, the British Green Party's share of the vote peaked at 15 per cent in 1989 and since then has fallen substantially. Nevertheless, in the 1992 General Election one Green MP was elected. He was a joint Green Party/Plaid Cymru candidate in a Welsh constituency (Vidal 1992). One explanation for these mixed trends may be that interest in Green political parties has waned in 'lead' states because of the advances already made and the emergence of new issues onto the agenda, but that the green parties in 'lag' states are continuing to improve their positions as the electorate still perceives a need for action. Moreover, in the environmental lead states all mainstream political parties have incorporated environmental issues into their platforms. This seems to be borne out by Porritt and Winner's analysis of the state of European Green Parties in 1988 (Porritt and Winner 1988: 217).

There are now green political parties in every east European country and they have been very active in the debates over the future direction of their countries (Jordan 1991). As French notes:

> Although the Green Parties did not do as well as initially expected in the Spring 1990 elections, their loss is in some sense a measure of the movement's success: virtually all the competing political parties had strong environmental platforms. For many parties, however, including a clause on environmental degradation in the platform was simply another way of criticising the old regime.
>
> (French 1991: 105)

This means that an important role for the political parties, as it is for green pressure groups, is to ensure that the new governments stick to their environmental promises.

Thus, it does appear that there is considerable environmental activity at the substate level as evidenced through the activities of the green consumer, pressure group activities and Green Party agendas. According to Haas:

> Despite the recent emergence of Green Parties throughout Europe, actual governmental policies for environmental protection and for international co-operation preceded this mass mobilization of public opinion.
>
> (Haas 1992: 45)

Nevertheless the activity at this level has forced governments and the EC to act on some problems and is vital for keeping environmental issues on the agenda, for publicising issues and generally maintaining momentum. Moreover, individuals, through their actions (e.g. green consumerism) can achieve changes that a government would find it difficult to legislate for because of opposition from industry.

ENVIRONMENTAL DIPLOMACY

Thus far it is member states of the European Community and European Free Trade Area (EFTA) who have played active roles in environmental diplomacy. The east European states are as yet focused on internal environmental issues. However, according to ZumBrunnen:

> With such large production of industrial pollutants, eastern Europe contributes significantly to the build-up of trace gases in the atmosphere, and given the projected natural and social impacts, these countries will not be able to escape all of the deleterious effects. Thus, it is clear that the states of eastern Europe will have to play important roles in the international scientific and political discussions on global environmental issues.
>
> (ZumBrunnen 1992: 88–9)

It is instructive to examine two international negotiations on key environmental issues; the negotiations over ozone depletion and global warming/climate change. The former issue resulted in a convention and subsequent protocols whilst the latter is still being negotiated. The west European states have played leading (though different) roles in these two negotiations.

The issue of ozone depletion was first placed on the international agenda in 1978 by the United States. Evidence was mounting that the ozone layer – which protects the earth from harmful ultraviolet radiation – was becoming depleted, in part because of extensive use of CFCs. The EC was the major producer of CFCs at 40 per cent of global production, whilst the USA produced 30 per cent of world supplies. The United States was much more willing to act on the issue and urged the EC to respond to the problem by reducing CFC production, but the EC was unresponsive, primarily because of opposition from Britain, France and Germany, all major producers of CFCs. The United States introduced unilateral restrictions on the use of CFCs in aerosols and urged the EC to do the same. However, the EC was only willing to call on members to reduce voluntarily non-essential aerosol use by 30 per cent of their 1976 production figure by 1982 (Rowlands 1992).

After the failure of these bilateral negotiations, multilateral negotiations began in Vienna in 1982. However, it was not until the 1985 Geneva Convention on Protection of the Ozone layer that agreement seemed likely. The Convention was important because the EC and other signatories admitted that there was a problem, and it contained a call for the negotiation of protocols to restrict the use of CFCs. The first of these was signed in Montreal in 1987. Between the Vienna Convention and the Montreal Protocol, the EC underwent a change of heart on the issue. This was due to waning opposition from Britain, France and Germany, public pressure on governments to agree (spurred by new information on a hole in the ozone layer) and successful bureaucratic battling by the European Commission to take a more active role on external environmental issues (Jachtenfuchs 1990). By 1989 the EC had taken the lead on the issue and decided to move unilaterally to eliminate CFC use completely by the year 2000. Following this announcement, the USA agreed to do the same.

The international negotiations on global warming are much more complicated than those on ozone depletion because all states are producers of substances that are thought to contribute to the 'greenhouse gases' which trap heat around the earth (carbon dioxide, methane, CFCs, etc.). Moreover, the scientific evidence about climate change and global warming is far from conclusive. There is also a distinct north–south element to this negotiation because many sources of energy are implicated in global warming, and developing nations fear that they may be expected to forgo development in the name of saving the planet. The first international conference on 'The Changing Atmosphere' was held in Canada in 1988. The closing declaration urged that a comprehensive global convention be negotiated as a framework for protocols on protection of the atmosphere.

This call was endorsed by the United Nations General Assembly in 1988. The UN also requested the UNEP and World Meteorological Organisation (WMO) through the Intergovernmental Panel on Climate Change (IPCC) to begin work towards a climate convention. There followed a series of international conferences and meetings, at which it became obvious that the United States, supported by Japan and the Soviet Union, were reluctant to enter specific negotiations on a climate convention.

At the 1990 World Climate Conference held in Geneva, common interests emerged between the United States, Soviet Union and the states of the South, in opposition to EFTA states. The eighteen European states were pressing for tough targets to be set for the stabilisation of carbon dioxide emissions. The USA and the Soviet Union were opposed because both are major producers of carbon dioxide and were concerned about the costs of converting industry. The states of the South were concerned that these targets would hamper their industrial development. This 'unholy alliance' of the largest producers and would-be consumers was able to block European moves. The United States delegation successfully argued that the concluding declaration should contain only a general call for emissions reductions (Prager 1992: 10).

Subsequent negotiations have seen the United States continuing to fight against tough emissions targets and the EC pushing the case for them. In November 1990 the IPCC's final report was presented at the Second World Climate Conference in Geneva. The delegates there confirmed a timetable of having a convention on climate change ready for signing at the 1992 Earth Summit. Thus far about 150 states have signed the convention and it should consequently come into force within the next two years.

In negotiations on ozone depletion the European states were initially reluctant to act and were pushed along by the United States. By contrast, in negotiations on climate change/global warming, it has been the European states pushing along the United States. An examination of these negotiations points to an important trend; that environmental negotiations are becoming just another type of international negotiation and therefore subject to diplomatic manoeuvring and the primacy of *raison d'etat* rather than being treated as an urgent international problem which overrides their individual interests.

There have been various regional initiatives to reduce transboundary pollution problems. The dependency of much of eastern Europe upon indigenous, low quality brown coal contributes to air pollution and acid precipitation (rain). Acid rain has caused extensive damage to forests in eastern Europe, Finland, Luxembourg, the Netherlands, Switzerland and (West) Germany. Although east European states are not the only culprits (West Germany's coal-fired power plants have exacerbated the problem), their outdated industrial plants with little or no pollution controls are a major problem. One response has been for those states receiving acid rain to contribute to the clean-up:

> Finland and Sweden both apparently believe that it will be economically efficient and ecologically sound for them to provide Eastern European industries with financial and technical pollution abatement assistance so that they might reduce their own acid pollution damage costs.
>
> (ZumBrunnen 1992: 99)

There have also been agreements between Finland and Poland, and Sweden and Poland aimed at reducing transboundary pollution. However, as ZumBrunnen points out, as western European states have not as yet solved their own acid rain production problems, there is less incentive to help eastern Europe.

Work has been undertaken on transboundary pollution by the Economic Commission for Europe (ECE). Under its auspices three air pollution reduction protocols have been signed. Several of the east European states who are signatories to these agreements lack the necessary technology to meet the agreed air pollution reduction targets. This shows the necessity for technology transfers to be included in international agreements. Some members of the Conference on Security and Cooperation in Europe (CSCE) have also requested that the ECE begin work on a transboundary water pollution treaty. In 1992 a Baltic Marine Ecology Convention was signed. This aims to protect the marine environment and undertake an action plan to reduce pollution in areas around the Baltic Sea (Reuter 1992).

It is clear from this discussion of global environmental diplomacy that the issue is being treated as just another negotiation between sovereign states (even though the problems do not respect sovereignty) rather than as a new and vital issue. However, this does not seem to be the case at the system level where there is more recognition of interdependence and willingness to act.

ENVIRONMENTALISM AND DEVELOPMENT

The debate over the relationship between development and the environment is a crucial issue for the states of eastern Europe, and still of relevance for the states of western Europe. The debate has become entangled with discussions about the most effective means of achieving development and the role of state planning within that.

It cannot be denied that the model of economic development adopted by the communist governments of eastern Europe took a heavy toll on the environment. This is a consequence of industry's gross inefficiency. According to French:

> Open-hearth steel manufacturing and other outdated, inefficient technologies are still widely used in East European and Soviet industries. On average, these countries use 50–100 per cent more energy than the United States to produce a dollar of gross domestic product and 100–300 per cent more than Japan.
>
> (French 1991: 95)

As George noted, the only constraints on environmental destruction were the far lower levels of private consumption than the west (George 1990a: 114).

Soon after the revolutions in the east, the new governments were involved in debates over the future directions of their economies. These were debates over whether to follow light green or dark green programmes. The former involves a moderated form of capitalism involving environmental legislation and government safeguards on the environment. Dark green solutions are far more radical and say that environmental degradation has been caused by over-consumption and that the only possible solution is a fundamental change in the relationship between people and the environment. This solution involves a move back to an organic way of life, away from industrialisation and consumerism. In reality, the debate was settled in the polls (with the poor showing of green parties) and the new east European governments have favoured a capitalist form of development, but with greater awareness of environmental issues. It should be noted that this is the model now followed by environmental 'lead' states, but it has still not been sufficient to effectively tackle the full gamut of environmental problems.

As noted above, many east European states are undertaking environmental clean-up operations. However, these will cause short-term economic and social dislocations. For example, the commitment to clean up industry threatens jobs at a time when unemployment is climbing steeply. Such a move could lead to civil unrest, the last thing that the new governments want. Additionally, the clean-up operation is likely to be very expensive. For instance, Poland's Environment Minister has estimated that improving the situation will cost $20 billion over the next ten to twenty years. Similarly, the former Czechoslovakian government believed that they needed to spend $23.7 billion on pollution control over the next fifteen years. At a time of extreme economic dislocation it will be difficult for states to plough the necessary funds into environmental improvement. Nevertheless, French provides a compelling case for environmental improvement:

> Throughout the region, however, cleaning up the environment is by no means a luxury. Though precise figures are hard to come by, economists estimate that environmental degradation is costing Poland 10–20 per cent of its gross national product (GNP) every year and Czechoslovakia, 5–7 per cent . . . investments in environmental protection are thus virtually guaranteed to provide economic benefits.
>
> (French 1991: 94)

One of the first moves towards capitalism has been the privatisation of land, resources and industry. Privatisation is a classic response to the 'tragedy of the commons' (Hardin 1968). However, as the example of western Europe shows, environmental problems do not disappear with privatisation alone. Within the states of eastern Europe there is now a debate going on over the priority to be given to the environment as opposed to development, with many people wishing to reap the consumer rewards of capitalism (Schwarz 1990).

In the west, faith was originally expressed in the ability of the market to advance the cause of environmentalism (Stavins 1989), however, there is now a fierce debate raging over the efficacy of voluntarist approaches to environmental improvement. This is a dialogue currently being conducted between the member states of the EC over environmental legislation. Multinational companies and businesses within European states have by and large opposed the attempts of governments and international organisations to enact environmental legislation. This opposition has largely been justified on the basis of costs. Industry fears that if it is forced to obey environmental legislation, it will be unable to compete in the market against industries which operate in unregulated areas.

The World Bank and the IMF have, since the 1980s, increasingly employed environmental criteria when making loan decisions (Postel and Flavin 1991: 174; Cartwright 1989). Thus far, primary consideration has been given to the effects of these changes on the states of the South, but they obviously also have implications for the development of the east European states (Montagon 1989). This is particularly true as both are now imposing 'green clauses' in the re-negotiation of debts. At the Earth Summit a Sustainable Development Commission was established. Part of its remit will be to move the IMF and World Bank closer to environmental accountability in their loan activities (Vidal 1992d). However, there is resistance within the World Bank to fundamental change (Postel and Flavin 1991: 174). A Global Environmental Facility (GEF) was set up in 1992, to be administered by the United Nations and the World Bank. The aim of the GEF is to help developing countries clean up the environment and meet international conventions of emissions reductions (Brummer 1992). Commercial banks are also increasingly considering environmental criteria when assessing loan applications (Cowe 1992).

The most important lending institution for the east European states is the European Bank for Reconstruction and Development (EBRD). According to Plant:

> there was strong pressure from environmentalist Non Government Organizations (NGOs) before the founding of the new bank . . . in 1990, to incorporate a particularly strong environmental mandate into its constitution and even to reflect the strength of environmental concerns about eastern Europe in its name.
>
> (Plant 1992: 137)

Although the latter attempt was unsuccessful, the mandate was included in the charter and this pressure for environmental responsibility from the outcome is bound to be reflected in the way that the new institution operates.

These changes in the lending policies of the Bank for Reconstruction and Development, the international aid agencies and the commercial banks have important consequences for the models of development undertaken in eastern Europe. This may mean that even if politicians in the east European states choose the quickest route to economic growth – which in all likelihood entails the highest economic costs – they may be prevented from following it by the need to satisfy the environmental conditions imposed by the lending authorities.

Another important type of actor which will influence the shape and form of any future development in east European states is the transnational corporation (TNC). The top 500 companies in the world together control 70 per cent of world trade, 80 per cent of foreign investment and 30 per cent of world GDP. They are the largest users of raw materials, the prime producers of goods that harm the environment (for example, the top 500 companies produce half the greenhouse gases of all global industries) and are also the major controllers of the science and technology which could play a valuable role in cleaning up the environment.

The ability of TNCs to influence the international system has been enhanced by the increasing moves to deregulation of the global economy. This is important in two respects. First, it may be that the type of development undertaken in east European states will be determined not by national governments but by the decisions made by TNCs. Secondly, because of their control of both production and end use, it may be that the level at which environmental issues should be tackled is through TNCs.

Some areas of international industry have already shown themselves interested in environmental issues (Elkington and Burke 1987). Business is increasingly keen to save energy and some companies are far ahead of national legislation on the environment. With the global shift to deregulation and private initiative the onus is firmly on business to incorporate environmental objectives into its ways of operating. A recent initiative has been the Business Council for Sustainable Development. This is an organisation composed of fifty of the biggest multinationals which is examining ways in which business can include social goals into its agenda (Cowe 1992a).

Nevertheless, we should not overestimate the environmental conversion of multinational companies. Several countries have worked to protect the interests of TNCs based within their territory. For example, before the UNCED conference there was a preparatory Committee meeting in New

York, essentially to set the agenda for Rio. At this meeting a proposal by China, the Group of Seventy-Seven (G77) and the Nordic countries that TNCs should accept environmental liability was defeated by Britain, the USA and Japan, all three of whom have many TNCs based in their countries (Vidal and Chaterjee 1992).

Given the interplay between environmental issues and economics noted above, the role of business is crucial – for good or ill. The picture is further confused by the changes currently occurring in the global political economy, which may hail a new era of regional bloc formation. If this is so, then this could have implications for environmental issues in that business may debunk to the areas with fewest environmental restrictions (and hence exacerbate 'free rider' problems) or more positively, may see obeying environmental legislation as a necessary prerequisite for gaining entry to lucrative markets. The EC has recognised the danger of 'ecological colonialism', i.e. the export of polluting industries, and is planning to establish an environmental code for investment in eastern Europe.

ENVIRONMENT AND SECURITY

Since the revolutions of 1989 undermined the Cold War ideas of what constituted a security threat, there has been an important debate conducted at two levels over the notion of security. At the first level there has been a debate within military and strategic circles about the types of threats faced by states in the contemporary international system. This debate encompasses arguments over the post-Cold War 'peace dividend' to be gained by cutting back the armed forces. Those seeking to defend the position and resources of the military have added on certain problems to the armed forces remit, for example, the war on drugs, coping with economic refugees and environmental security. It has also been suggested that the military be employed in cleaning up the environment (Deudney 1991; Theorin 1992), and that it has a role to play in data gathering on environmental problems (Gore 1992). These ideas are increasingly being reflected in both the spending plans of states and the ways in which security organisations are planning for the future.

The North Atlantic Treaty Organisation (NATO) has undertaken a fundamental review of security which it published in its November 1991 document 'The Alliance's New Strategic Concept' (NATO 1991: 3). It states the need for a broad approach to security which acknowledges that 'security and stability have political, economic, social and environmental elements as well as the indispensable defence element' (NATO 1991: 6). The new concept also encourages a greater use of the CSCE forum and acknowledges that migration, economic dislocation and environmental change may be security challenges that NATO has to face. However, the premise is that these threats will manifest themselves in a physical challenge on NATO countries. In this way, NATO has merely added to the list of issues that may cause conventional conflict, rather than re-thought its understanding of the nature of security.

The efforts of some to combine environmental issues with national security policy have led to debates in a second arena: academia. The debate has been conducted in two different ways. On the one hand, there are those who have sought to build onto existing concepts of security notions of environmental threat (Mathews 1989; Brown 1986; Buzan 1991; Gleick 1991). This has much in common with previous attempts to widen the notion of security to include socio-economic aspects (Tinbergen and Fischer 1987). On the other hand, are those who feel that the whole concept of security is in need of a radical overhaul because it is tied up with problematic concepts like sovereignty, national interest, etc. and should therefore not just be widened (Deudney 1991: 26).

This expanded concept of security has met opposition from those who feel that the two concepts are incompatible. Particularly interesting has been the contribution of Deudney, who argues that the likening of environmental problems to a national security issue has been a device used by environmentalists to concentrate attention on these issues. However, for Deudney, this clearly does not work as he argues that the threats from environmental problems are fundamentally different from traditional violent security threats (Deudney 1991: 24). Some of the major differences he identifies are: the threats are not often national in character, there is no intention involved in environmental problems and the organisations which deal with the two types of issues are very different. He also asserts that the likelihood of environmental problems resulting in conflict is very low, and discusses and dismisses four possible scenarios which have been suggested as likely to result in conflict. He concludes that 'Ecological degradation is not a threat to national security; rather environmentalism is a threat to national security attitudes and institutions' (Deudney 1991: 28). Deudney's argument can be taken further in respect to the type of thinking and planning necessitated by environmental degradation. In contrast to situations of military conflict, where security often was viewed as a zero-sum game (a loss for one state was a gain for another), environmental issues are often a zero-plus game in that an action by one state can benefit all. Although this exacerbates the free rider problem (Grubb 1990), the potential for cooperation is greater on this type of issue than any other. This type of zero-plus thinking is already in evidence in Europe in unilateral actions by Germany and the Netherlands to reduce carbon dioxide emissions (Pearce 1992: 65).

However, one less hopeful trend is also emerging. In traditional notions of security, worst case analysis was common, with the emphasis on capabilities rather than intentions. When examining environmental issues, however, it now appears to be the environmentalists who are adopting worst case analysis and governments who are resisting it. This is an ironic role reversal, particularly given the links between environmentalists and the peace movements – who saw their task as to move states away from worst case analysis.

In Europe the debate over the relationship between the environment and security will continue to be bifurcated. It seems unlikely that NATO, the Western European Union and individual states' military establishments will be willing to shed their new-found justifications for defending their budgets and maintaining the size of their forces.

CONCLUSIONS

Because there are such diverse elements within the environmental issue it will remain on the European agenda into the twenty-first century; as one aspect of the environment comes off the agenda another will appear to replace it. Moreover, the fact that the environment is tackled at four different levels – global, system, state, and substate – means that there is a constant interaction between the levels which keeps environmental issues alive. Each level receives momentum from the other levels and in turn provides momentum for the other levels. For example, the attention paid to the Earth Summit (global level) has reinforced interest at the substate level, which will impel states to continue to address environmental issues.

One of the important points highlighted by this review of environmental problems and debates is that it cannot be assumed that the answers to the dilemmas lie exclusively in any one level and that interactions between the levels are vital. Indeed, focusing on these four levels ignores what may be a key element in the environmental equation: the role of TNCs. These are the organisations which have control of both production and consumption and as such are an important level at which environmental issues should be tackled.

What conclusions can be reached about the key aspects of environmentalism discussed above? In terms of environmental diplomacy some interesting trends are emerging which suggest that the system level is the best one for tackling the more pervasive environmental problems. Agreement is more likely between a fairly homogeneous group of states, and it seems that once EC nations have reached agreement on an issue they then work effectively together at the global level and pull other states into agreements. Although this common front does not mean an abandonment of the normal pulling and hauling of diplomatic negotiation with other states, it does provide evidence of the transcending of the narrow perspectives of individual states and the forging of a real regional identity. Thus although the progress of environmental diplomacy to date points to the primacy of *raison d'etat*, this is less evident in EC stances. Moreover, the regional initiatives on pollution point to the increasing willingness of states to recognise interdependence and work together.

The model of economic development being employed by the former communist states of Europe shows the primacy of development over environmental issues. The environmental groups and green parties in these states are now fighting to keep green issues on the agenda. In this fight they will be assisted by the international lending institutions' employment of environmental criteria in loan decisions. Moreover, the desire of these new states to become accepted into the EC will also incline them towards environmental responsibility. The role of transnational corporations will also be crucial in determining production practices. There are two possible scenarios for the future of east European industries. First, there could be an influx of polluting industries into these states, to take advantage of the poor implementation of environmental legislation. Secondly, east European industries could face barriers to trading with the rest of Europe because of their poor environmental production practices. Both these scenarios suggest a period of economic dislocation and east–west friction over the relationship between environment and development. A worrying third scenario might also be considered: that TNCs choose to invest in the Third World and east European states are left struggling to develop.

The debate over environmental security seems set to remain in two different arenas: the realm of policy-making and that of academia. The course of policy is already set, with environmental threats being viewed as an added justification for the continued existence of NATO. Unfortunately, however, it seems that the worst-case thinking which propelled states to act during the Cold War is now largely absent from governmental approaches to environmental problems.

ACKNOWLEDGEMENT

The author would like to thank Dr Neil Carter of York University for his helpful comments on a draft of this chapter.

Chapter 8

The human rights and security agenda

Beyond non-intervention?

Nicholas Wheeler

INTRODUCTION

The Yugoslav conflict of 1991–2, like the case of the oppression of the Kurds in northern Iraq in early 1991, raises the fundamental question as to whether international society should legitimise humanitarian intervention where there are gross violations of human rights – caused by either state oppression and/or civil war – even though this challenges fundamental norms of sovereignty and non-intervention in the internal affairs of states. Through a case study of the responses of the Conference on Security and Cooperation in Europe (CSCE) and the European Community (EC) to the Yugoslav crisis, this chapter seeks to explore the boundaries of what constitutes legitimate intervention in post-Cold War Europe. It will be argued that strengthening the protection of human rights and minority rights in the new Europe is not only necessary on humanitarian grounds, but is also vital to future European security. This is not to negate the significance of humanitarian ethics, but it is to recognise that these considerations have to be coupled with motivations of national self-interest before governments will be willing to challenge the norm of non-intervention in the society of states. Hence, in focusing on west European responses to the Yugoslav crisis, an assessment will be made as to how far national self-interest and humanitarian considerations motivated these governments in their interventions in the crisis in 1991–2.

THE LEGITIMACY OF HUMANITARIAN INTERVENTION IN THE SOCIETY OF STATES

Despite the principle of non-intervention enshrined in Article 2 (7) of the United Nations Charter – this prohibits intervention in the internal affairs of states – the way a government treats its own people has become increasingly a legitimate object of international scrutiny in the post-war period. The following all bear testimony to the growing protection in international law of the right of individuals: the Nuremberg and Tokyo War Crimes Tribunals; the Universal Declaration of Human Rights; Articles 55 and 56 of the United Nations Charter; the international covenants on civil, political, economic and social rights; and the agreement in ECOSOC Resolution 1503 which allows individuals to petition the United Nations Sub-Commission on human rights when there are gross violations. This protection of individual human rights is most highly developed in the Council of Europe – which provides legal redress for individuals in member states through the machinery of the European Court of Human Rights – and the Conference on Security and Cooperation in Europe (CSCE).[1] The latter, although lacking a treaty base in international law, has made considerable progress in setting out standards for the protection of human rights in Europe (Vincent 1991: 248–50; Gardner 1991/92: 68–9).

The developments do suggest that a state's human rights policies no longer fall within the remit of Article 2 (7); but is it reasonable to consider the existing human rights regime as constituting a form of humanitarian intervention – given that it lacks enforcement power beyond that of moral censure and diplomatic condemnation – in international society? Enforcement action beyond this could take the form of diplomatic isolation, the use of coercive economic sanctions or even forcible intervention. Given that international society has shown no willingness in the past to legitimise humanitarian intervention on this scale, are there grounds for believing that it might be willing to do so in the future?

The idea that humanitarian intervention is a moral imperative is identified with the cosmopolitanist view of international relations. For the cosmopolitanist, what matters are the rights and duties that individuals have to each other by virtue of their common humanity; rights and duties which should not be diluted by the artificial barriers of state sovereignty and non-intervention. Human rights for cosmopolitanists are a security issue because the primary referent for security is not – as for realists – the security of states, but an emergent community of humankind (Linklater 1990: 8–33; Vincent 1986: 118–19). This idea of the security of individuals as indivisible echoes Kant's conviction that the violation of a right in one place should be felt everywhere. The age of electronic media has made this idea more of a reality; a few seconds of prime time television can send images of suffering and violence into the homes of millions across the globe.

In asserting that humankind should be sensitised to rights violations everywhere, cosmopolitanists recognise that prudential considerations cannot be ignored when deciding how to respond. Governments have a range of possible responses to human rights abuses: moral censure, diplomatic condemnation, economic sanctions and, in the last resort, forcible intervention. In deciding upon the latter – in cases of extreme human rights violations – governments have to consider the risk that armed humanitarian intervention might drive large wedges in an international order based on sovereign states and the norm of non-intervention (Vincent 1986: 113–18; Morris 1991: 4–9). Against this, cosmopolitanists would argue that the general priority accorded by governments to order over justice should be questioned where great injustice is embodied in the existing order, and where a judgement is made that pursuing justice will not destroy the foundations of international order (Bull 1977: 86–98). Thus, as Vincent and Wilson note, what is sought is not a general licence for forcible humanitarian intervention since this would threaten the bases of international order, but a suspension of the norm of non-intervention in those extreme cases where genocide or massive violations of human rights are taking place, and where prudence does not rule out forcible intervention (Vincent and Wilson, 1992). Since for the cosmopolitanist, every life is of equal moral worth – irrespective of national identity (Linklater 1990) – the moral dilemma facing governments is to balance the costs of humanitarian intervention, in terms of the possible loss of lives, as against the expected benefits in terms of the relief of humanitarian suffering.

Set against the cosmopolitanist there is the realist who sees international politics as taking place in a moral void where notions of moral and political community are bounded by the state, with the latter having the supreme responsibility to provide for the security of its citizens. For realists, intervention on human rights grounds is a misnomer since lives are not all of equal moral worth. As a consequence, states will not risk the security of their citizens to try to relieve the humanitarian suffering of others. Realists argue that the problem with legitimising humanitarian intervention is that in the absence of a universal consensus on notions of justice in world politics, this will issue a licence for intervention which will destroy the foundations of international order (Franck and Rodley 1973: 275–305; Morris 1991: 4–9). Realists like Henry Kissinger and Hans Morgenthau are not dismissive of human rights concerns, but they are mindful that they do not get in the way of the management of the diplomatic game. Hence, for this school of realists, foreign policy should be divested of moral crusades and based on a shared code of external conduct rather than on the search for legitimising principles that reflect each state's own domestic values: the latter being a recipe for chaos and disorder (Kissinger 1957: 328–30).

The problem with Kissinger's argument of divorcing the internal politics of a state, including its human rights policies, from relations between states is that the former seem to impinge more crucially on the latter than is given credit for in some realist accounts. The next section seeks to explore the linkages between human rights and international security in relation to the security problems of post-Cold War Europe.

HUMAN RIGHTS AND INTERNATIONAL SECURITY

Stanley Hoffmann has suggested that 'no state should be able to claim that the way a state treats its own citizens is its sovereign right if this is likely to threaten international peace and security' (Hoffmann 1991). He suggests that the very 'conditions that lead to tyranny and large-scale violations of human rights at home sooner or later spill over into a search for enemies abroad' (Hoffmann 1991). This is the counter-argument to the Kissinger view, and it was one which found favour with many academics and government officials during the Cold War in relation to the Soviet Union. Supporters of this view would point to the fact that it took internal liberalisation in the Soviet Union to produce the accelerating détente of the late 1980s, and the subsequent end of the Cold War.

Despite these claims, it would be unwise to posit too automatic a linkage between oppressive internal behaviour and aggressive external behaviour. There are many examples of internally repressive states which were cautious in their external behaviour such as Stalin's Russia, or the Latin American states in the post-war period, while liberal democracy is no guarantee of civilised behaviour abroad as can be seen from US support for all manner of repressive regimes since 1945. Nevertheless, it would be foolish to deny that there does sometimes exist a connection between internally repressive behaviour and external aggressiveness. Iraq's wars of aggression may be viewed as a recent example of this linkage between internal and external behaviour, while it will be suggested later in the chapter that Serbian leader, Slobodan Milosevic, also fits the pattern of leaders and elites exporting domestic violence internationally.

It is not only the dangers of a direct connection between internal repressiveness and external violence that demonstrates the link between human rights and international security; there is also the risk that intra-state violence will spill over national borders. This might take the form of refugee movements, regional economic dislocation and even interstate conflict itself. Domestic conflicts may lead to outside intervention, as happened during the Cold War, when the US and Soviet Union intervened through proxy forces in numerous Third World conflicts, but this risk is most acute where a government threatens a minority group within its borders who are co-nationals of a neighbouring state.

Minority rights problems are not confined to the ex-communist states of Europe, but developing a system for the protection of minority rights lies at the heart of the security challenges facing European states in the post-Cold War era (Mayall 1992: 19–35). The diverse ethnic and nationality groups which make up the patchwork quilt of the post-communist states do not as yet have the same sense of civic identity or citizenship found in the more mature democracies of western Europe. As a result, minorities are vulnerable to those leaders and groups who are fearful as to their loyalty and/or who are manipulating nationalist feeling in an effort to distract attention from past and present domestic shortcomings. Similarly, the way other states treat their minorities has become a live political issue for those governments – such as Hungary and Russia – which have millions of co-nationals living in neighbouring states. Consequently, in the absence of an effective international system for protecting minority rights in Europe, it seems that there will be an increasing risk of interstate violence as governments are pressurised by their publics to protect their kith and kin in neighbouring states. Thus, while west European governments and public opinion may well feel an ethic of responsibility to protect the rights of individuals and groups in the post-communist states, they also have a long-term security interest in providing mechanisms for the international protection of minority rights.

HUMAN RIGHTS, SECURITY AND THE CSCE

The idea that there is a relationship between the protection of human rights and international security can be seen at work in the development of the CSCE process. Member states signed up in the Helsinki Final Act of 1975 to a form of words which articulated a clear linkage between human rights and international security. Indeed, the end of the Cold War might be seen in part as a victory for the human rights provisions of the CSCE, since the latter played a role in de-legitimising the Stalinist elites of eastern Europe.

The Helsinki Final Act embodied several core principles: sovereign equality and non-intervention; the right to self-determination of all peoples; and respect for individual and minority rights (protection of minority rights being the only one of the CSCE's core principles which is not also found in the United Nations Charter). If a key part of the Helsinki Final Act of 1975 was the setting out of rules of the road for the regulation of interstate relations with prohibition of the use of force to change existing territorial borders central to the CSCE process – the western powers and neutral states vigorously argued that human rights were now a matter of legitimate international concern, and hence not prohibited by the non-intervention principle, and that intervention in contravention of Article 2 (7) of the United Nations Charter was to be defined, as John Vincent notes, as 'dictatorial interference – the implication being that lesser forms of "interference" were not illegal' (Vincent 1991: 250).

The Soviet Union did agree to the human rights provisions of the CSCE in return for the west's according legitimacy to the post-war division of Europe, especially the inviolability of the borders of the German Democratic Republic. However, in retrospect, it seems unthinkable that Moscow expected the human rights provisions of the CSCE to be as significant as they turned out to be, believing no doubt that the norm of non-intervention would enable it to walk away from discussion of the detailed implementation of the human rights provisions of the Final Act. Certainly, when its record of compliance in the human rights field was raised at the CSCE follow-up meeting in Belgrade and later Madrid, Moscow sought to invoke the principle of non-intervention. As Vincent notes, Moscow did not reject the idea that human rights were a matter of international concern, but it did resist the west's right to monitor its implementation of agreements, arguing that it was the sovereign responsibility of states to implement the human rights provisions of the Helsinki Final Act (Vincent 1991: 250). Thus, from the outset, the CSCE was plagued by debates as to what constitutes the boundaries of permissible humanitarian intervention in the society of states.

As the Cold War gradually gave way to an accelerating *détente* in the late 1980s, the Soviet Union's attitude, and that of its eastern bloc allies, softened on the question of international monitoring of the human rights provisions of the CSCE. Pressures for internal liberalisation in the east, which were helped in no small part by the work of Helsinki monitoring groups like Charter 77, and which had been dramatically speeded up by Gorbachev's 'new thinking', led the Soviet Union and east European governments to accept in the concluding document of the Vienna CSCE follow-up meeting in November 1989, that the implementation of a state's human rights obligations should be open to the scrutiny and monitoring of other CSCE states (Vincent 1991: 250–51).

The signing of the Paris Charter, a year after the collapse of the east European communist regimes, codified the growing achievements of the CSCE in the human rights field. Especially important in the Paris Charter was a detailed set of provisions for the protection of minority rights since it was increasingly recognised within the CSCE that protecting minority rights would be critical to future European security. At Paris, governments also agreed to further institutionalise the CSCE, creating a permanent Secretariat to be based in Prague and a Conflict Prevention Centre (CPC) to be based in Vienna. A Committee of Senior Officials (CSO) was also set up that would do the preparatory work for meetings of a CSCE Council which would meet at least twice yearly at Foreign Minister level.

Yet, while there was much optimism as to the future role of the CSCE as a forum for conflict resolution after the signing of the Paris Charter, these hopes were dashed by the Soviet crack-down in Lithuania in early 1991. In the face of this violation of CSCE human rights principles, the neutral states plus former Czechoslovakia, Hungary and Poland called for an urgent special CSCE meeting to discuss Soviet military actions in the Baltics, activating the articles agreed in the 1990 Vienna Document which allow states to ask for an explanation of why signatory states have not upheld their human rights obligations. This call for a special CSCE meeting (requiring unanimity) was fully supported by EC member states and NATO, but it was rejected by the Soviet Union as representing interference in its internal affairs, and therefore in violation of the CSCE principle of non-intervention. The Lithuanian crisis demonstrated the fundamental problem which faces the CSCE in the human rights field. It can set standards, but it does not have the ability to enforce these on member states.

Frustrated by the ability of one state to veto the convening of a special CSCE meeting, there was growing interest among west European governments and the US in strengthening the CSCE's interventionary powers. This led to the CSCE adopting in June 1991 an 'emergency mechanism' for dealing with crises.

With EC member states, and especially Germany taking the lead, the CSCE Council, meeting in Berlin in June 1991, agreed that an emergency meeting could be triggered without the consent of one member state provided that there were thirteen or more of the then thirty-four member states in favour. This meeting took place against the background of the developing crisis in Yugoslavia. However, Moscow was very reluctant to allow any development which might lead to CSCE interference in its own internal affairs, especially fearful here of possible CSCE intervention in support of the self-determination of the Baltic republics. The Soviet Union was only persuaded to come on board when it was agreed that once an emergency meeting had been called, any subsequent action would have to proceed on the basis of consensus. The Berlin document states that emergency meetings must apply 'the principle of non-intervention in internal affairs . . . when it decides on action' (*The Independent* 1991). Although this appeared highly restrictive, those in favour of extending the CSCE's interventionary capacities argued that this left room for debate as to what constitutes 'internal affairs' and legitimate intervention (echoing a long-standing debate within the CSCE). Nevertheless, the extent of the

CSCE's willingness to legitimise humanitarian intervention was to be severely tested by the Yugoslav crisis, which confronted it with a conflict between several of its core legitimising principles.

THE CSCE'S RESPONSES TO THE YUGOSLAV CRISIS

The international dimension of the Yugoslav crisis was triggered by the Croatian and Slovenian declarations of independence on 25 June 1991, declarations which in themselves posed a threat to CSCE and United Nations principles of maintaining the territorial integrity of states. However, since the right of all peoples to self-determination is also a key CSCE and UN principle, here was a situation where two of the CSCE's core legitimising principles were apparently in conflict. The Yugoslav situation was further complicated in that at the heart of the crisis was the issue of minority rights. What seems to have sparked the violence between Serbs and Croats was the determination of the Serbian minority in Croatia to remain part of Yugoslavia – and the willingness of the nationalist Serbian leadership in Belgrade – and the Serbian dominated Yugoslav Peoples Army (YPA) – to help those Serbs living in Croatia remain part of the Yugoslav state (Gow and Freedman, 1992: 1). Here, the increasing insensitivity of the Croatian republican government of Franjo Tudjman (elected in 1990) to the rights of Croatia's Serb minority was a major factor in the outbreak of armed conflict between Serbs and Croats.

Faced with such a complex situation, the vast majority of CSCE governments – crucially EC member states and the US – took the view that they could not support the secessionist demands of the republics of Croatia and Slovenia (Austria, Hungary and Germany were the most sympathetic to these aspirations). Instead, the CSCE issued a statement in support of the territorial integrity of Yugoslavia and respect for human rights and minority rights within all the republics of the Yugoslav federation. This position can be seen as the lowest common denominator that the then thirty-four member states of the CSCE could reach. Many states, especially the Soviet Union, were very fearful of the precedent that recognition of Croatia and Slovenia might set for their own restive nationalities. Although this did reflect the parochial concerns of multinational states fearful of triggering secessionist movements within their own borders, it might also be seen as an expression of a more general fear among states that supporting self-determination in this case might unleash a wave of secessionist movements which would challenge the stability of existing borders in the society of states.

Nevertheless, in not initially supporting the right to self-determination of the republics of Croatia and Slovenia, international society may have unintentionally sent a green light to Milosevic, and the Generals of the YPA, that they could get away with their actions which through 1991 amounted to the re-drawing of Yugoslavia's internal borders by force (Gow 1992: 305–6). The use of force by the YPA and Serb irregulars represented a massive violation of CSCE human rights principles. Additionally, given that the inter-republican borders of Yugoslavia form part of the Helsinki Final Act (Gow 1992: 308), it also threatened the CSCE and United Nations principle of non-use of force to change existing territorial borders.

The CSCE met several times under its new 'emergency mechanism' during the summer of 1991 to try to find a solution to the growing violence that was accompanying the break-up of Yugoslavia. But since it continued to persist with the fiction that Yugoslavia was a sovereign state, it could not act – beyond moral and political censure, without the consent of the nominal Yugoslav government. There was no consensus in the CSCE to suspend the unanimity rule, over-turn the non-intervention principle, single out Serbia as the principal aggressor, and apply effective sanctions against the Milosevic government.

In the face of the CSCE's problems in dealing with the Yugoslav crisis, Germany's then Foreign Minister, Hans Dietrich Genscher, took the lead in arguing that the CSCE should be further strengthened in its ability to protect human rights and minority rights. This led to agreement in September 1991 at the Moscow conference on the Human Dimension of the CSCE among the now 38 CSCE states – the Baltic states having joined in the aftermath of the failed Soviet coup in August 1991 – that, with the support of five other states, a government could initiate the sending of a human rights mission into another state to monitor its compliance with its human rights commitments (Moscow meeting of the Conference on the Human Dimension of the CSCE, 10 September–4 October 1991). Although the post-coup Soviet government was willing to accept measures which previously it had resisted, it should not be thought that CSCE member states were over-turning the unanimity principle since the key weakness of the Moscow accord was that it did not specify what happened to a state which refused to cooperate with a CSCE mission, or deny it entry. Germany had argued that there ought to be provision for sanctions if the violating state resisted CSCE intervention, but this was too strong for many governments, fearful that their own human rights record might come under the scrutiny of the CSCE at a future date. Once again, the need for consensus among thirty-eight governments weakened the final accord to that of the lowest common denominator.

West European states, with Germany again taking the lead, did secure, at the 1991 Rome Summit, the support of NATO member states for the idea that the CSCE's rule of unanimity be suspended in 'cases of clear, gross and uncorrected violations' of CSCE human rights principles (Rome Declaration of Peace and Cooperation, November 1991: 3). This was adopted by CSCE foreign ministers meeting in Prague in January 1992 (this meeting also saw the joining of the CSCE by the former republics of the Soviet Union), and endorsed by heads of government at the Helsinki Summit of July of that year. But on the question of sanctions, the CSCE was only prepared to endorse 'political declarations or other political steps to apply outside the territory of the state concerned' (Meeting of the CSCE Council, Prague, January 1992). Yet, the weakness of these powers can be seen in the fact that the fifty-two member states (Croatia, Slovenia and Bosnia joining the CSCE at Helsinki) of the CSCE could not even agree in July 1992 to expel Serbia and Montenegro (the rump Yugoslav state) for their violation of the organisation's core principles. Agreement could only be reached on suspending Serbia and Montenegro from inheriting the seat of the former Yugoslavia.

As James Gow and Lawrence Freedman point out, the lesson of the Yugoslav crisis for the CSCE is the urgency of 'political early warning and a readiness to act decisively while a conflict is still simmering, rather than waiting until it boils over' (Gow and Freedman, 1992: 2). Had concerted international pressure been applied in the months preceding Croatia and Slovenia's declarations of independence – on the basis of the CSCE's formula of keeping Yugoslavia together as a single entity with increased protection for human rights and minority rights – it is possible that violence might have been prevented, or at least the subsequent carnage considerably reduced, but such intervention was not forthcoming (Greene 1992: 3). Moreover, had the CSCE been an effective protector of minority rights, it would have acted in response to Milosevic's oppression of the Albanian minority in Kosovo and the Hungarian minority in Vojvodina in the late 1980s (Freedman and Gow, 1992: 1). The US Congress did seek to cut off aid to the federal government in Belgrade in the hope that the latter might prevail on the Serbian republic to stop its oppression of human rights in Kosovo. United States bi-lateral aid was quite limited, but Congress also wanted the USA to push for the withdrawal of International Monetary Fund (IMF) and World Bank finance from Yugoslavia. Despite this, the Bush Administration accepted the Federal President's plea that the Yugoslav people should not be made to suffer for Serbia's abuse of human rights, and that denial of IMF loans might speed up economic breakdown and hasten civil war (Gow 1992: 306).

In retrospect, it is possible to argue that Serbia's abuse of human rights at home posed a threat to international security. Had western states placed Yugoslavia in diplomatic isolation and imposed economic sanctions against it for Serbia's behaviour in Kosovo, however unfair this might have been to non-Serbs, it is possible that far from speeding up the violent break-up of Yugoslavia, such an international response might have fostered a more moderate government than the Milosevic regime – or at least more moderate behaviour by that regime. Indeed, the latter's behaviour seems to confirm Hoffmann's proposition that the way a government acts within its borders provides a signal as to how it might act towards others. It also confirms the proposition, which lies at the heart of the CSCE, that strengthening the protection of human rights is co-extensive with the provision of wider European security. The problem for the CSCE is that while it has the legal right to monitor the human rights behaviour of governments, most of its members are very reluctant to give it the ability to enforce respect for human rights, fearing that such powers might be used to legitimise humanitarian intervention in their internal affairs in the future.[2]

If the CSCE lacks the ability to enforce its human rights standards, it seems that EC member states – by virtue of their political and economic muscle – have an increasingly important role to play in persuading governments to protect human rights and minority rights in post-Cold War Europe. But how far are EC states willing to go in challenging the norm of non-intervention where there are gross violations of human rights or minority rights in the new Europe?

THE EC AND THE PROTECTION OF HUMAN RIGHTS

The EC is a determined supporter of democratic values in the society of states. It restricts its membership to those states which exhibit both domestic and international civility, and is increasingly using its growing political and economic weight in international society to strengthen democratic values. The EC has two key instruments at its disposal for strengthening the protection of human rights in post-Cold War Europe: first, economic leverage and secondly, the weapon of diplomatic recognition. Both of these were tried in the Yugoslav crisis.

As discussed earlier, EC member states initially adopted the position that Yugoslavia should remain a single political entity. Germany was least happy with this policy, being the most supportive of the rights of Croatia and Slovenia to self-determination. Despite this, to maintain a common EC position, Germany accepted the collective view that republics which seceded from the federation would not receive economic aid and beneficial trade concessions (over 50 per cent of Yugoslavia's trade was with the EC), but that these would be readily available if there was a political settlement based on the maintenance of a single Yugoslav state (Salmon 1992: 248–9). However, few in Yugoslavia were thinking about the state of the economy in June 1991, and the EC's promise of economic assistance – if a constitutional settlement could be found – came too late to quell the rising violence in the country. Indeed, the outbreak of armed conflict in Slovenia, and the intensification of the violence in Croatia in July/August 1991, signalled the failure of the EC's common policy of holding Yugoslavia together.

There were four key motivating factors driving EC member states during the subsequent Yugoslav crisis of 1991–2. First, there was the determination to demonstrate that EC member states acting through European Political Cooperation (EPC) could pursue a common foreign and security policy (CFSP). This partly reflected a desire to do better than over the Gulf War, but it was also a recognition that historically the Balkans was a region over which leading west European states had quarrelled; there was a determination that this crisis would not lead to competitive inter-ventions by EC member states. Secondly, and linked to the first point, there was the fear that the Yugoslav crisis might spill across borders, and that this would threaten a wider conflagration in the region, bringing with it regional economic collapse and an uncontrollable flow of refugees across the borders of western Europe. Thirdly, there was the determination to ensure that none of the local actors in the conflict were seen to have prospered from the use of force, since this might set a dangerous precedent in post-Cold War Europe. Finally, there was the moral responsibility that was felt among western governments and public opinion at the scale of the humanitarian suffering caused by the war in Yugoslavia.

Through the summer of 1991, the EC, with CSCE backing, tried to play an impartial mediating role between the warring parties. But the violence continued to escalate with Croatia ordering a full mobilisation of forces, and with elements of the YPA and Serb irregulars effectively driving out non-Serbs to create Serbian enclaves – the dreadful 'ethnic cleansing'. As a result of this, there was a growing sense of outrage in western public opinion that Europe ought to be doing more to end the bloodshed in Yugoslavia.

The EC decided to intervene more decisively within the civil war. It asked Lord Carrington to chair a peace conference which would explore the bases for a settlement of the conflict. Attached to the peace conference was an arbitration commission tasked with providing legal expertise. With the backing of EC member states, Carrington proposed a general settlement which held out the promise of independence for those republics seeking it, and which included guarantees for the protection of human rights and minority rights. Not surprisingly, the Milosevic government, and the Serb minority in Croatia, refused to accept the peace plan on the grounds that Serbs outside of Serbia would not accept the status of a minority (Weller 1992: 589–92; Zametica 1992: 62–3). However, with five out of the six republics accepting the EC plan, Serbia was isolated. It was given until 28 October 1991 to accept the plan, with the clear signal sent that if it refused, the EC would go ahead with the other five republics, offering them economic support and eventually diplomatic recognition. In the face of continuing Serbian defiance, the EC imposed a range of economic sanctions against Belgrade in early November 1991 (Freedman and Gow, 1992: 24–9).[3]

The use of economic weapons by EC member states might be judged a failure in the Yugoslav crisis, but it has to be remembered that by the time the EC became seriously involved, the scope for economic pressures was severely limited. Once armed conflict had occurred, the last thing the warring parties were worrying about was the long-term state of their economies. Had it been possible for the EC and other western governments to apply economic coercion against the Serbian republic for its oppression of minority rights, and to employ a mix of carrots and sticks to pressurise the Croatian republic into treating its Serb minority better, it is possible that the Yugoslav war might have been averted. Since concerted international pressure was never effectively applied against Serbia or Croatia, it is impossible to say whether a more determined use of the economic weapon, and a more activist policy of anticipatory humanitarian intervention, would have averted the slide into violence. Against this, the Balkans is an extremely complex area in which to try to manipulate economic rewards and punishments, and given the bitter ethnic conflicts which have been unleashed (having been dormant since the Second World War) by the war in Yugoslavia, it might be that even anticipatory humanitarian intervention would not have prevented war.

Nevertheless, as Edward Mortimer notes, the promise of substantial economic aid and special association agreements for the economically poor post-communist states does provide the EC with an important policy lever for securing compliance with CSCE rules and principles (Mortimer 1992). One of the most important of these carrots is the prospect of eventual entry into the EC itself (Heisbourg 1992). But while economic success is the best guarantee of long-term stability and prosperity in Europe, it can be agreed with François Heisbourg that 'ethnic and territorial conflicts do not tend to wait long enough for economic measures to take hold' (Heisbourg 1991).

The second weapon in the EC's arsenal for protecting human rights is diplomatic recognition, although like economic means of influence, this carries with it no guarantee of success. EC member states can make diplomatic recognition conditional on acceptance of CSCE human rights provisions, but they cannot turn political recognition on and off like a tap, as they more easily can in the case of economic aid. Despite this, the promise of recognition can be used by the EC to try to persuade those who want to join the society of states, that membership is seen to carry with it obligations to protect human rights and minority rights. This can be seen as part of a wider attempt by the western liberal democracies to create a new standard of legitimacy in international society based on respect for human rights (Jackson 1992: 33–8). In the Yugoslav case, the question of recognition was more complicated for a civil war was in progress, and the debate was over whether internationalisation of the conflict would escalate or dampen the violence.

By early September 1991, the Germans were keen to recognise Croatia and Slovenia as independent states, believing that this would make the Serbs more amenable to compromise, since by this action the Serbian dominated YPA would have been turned into an invading force. This move was resisted by the British and French who feared that it would only stiffen the Serbs determination to carve out Serbian enclaves, fuel Croatian demands for European military assistance, and by raising the thorny problem of independence for Bosnia-Hercegovina, escalate the conflict to that republic (*The Economist* 1992: 39).

In an effort to avoid a direct clash over the issue, the European Council (the EC meeting at heads of government level) agreed in December 1991 that it would accord recognition to those existing Yugoslav republics which provided full guarantees for human rights and minority rights. The European Council asked its arbitration commission to investigate which of the Yugoslav republics had met these standards, but before it could report back, Bonn decided to unilaterally recognise Croatia and Slovenia. Some EC member states, especially Britain, were very unhappy with Bonn's unilateralism, since it seemed to make a mockery of ideas for a CFSP which had been agreed in the Maastricht Treaty. Nevertheless, to try to maintain some semblance of a common position, Bonn's partners fell into line, despite the EC's own arbitration commission finding that Croatia had not provided adequate guarantees for its Serbian minority (Salmon 1992: 252–3; Gow and Smith 1992: 34–6).

Having recognised Croatia and Slovenia, the EC found itself as Britain and France had feared, having to deal with the question of Bosnian independence. Bosnian Serbs rejected the demands of Croats and Muslims for independence, since they were determined not to live in a state dominated by the latter. They were strongly supported in this by Milosevic and the YPA, thus leading to a civil war between Bosnian Serb forces on the one hand, and Bosnian government troops (predominantly Muslim) on the other. John Zametica argues that before the EC recognised Bosnia as independent, there were no minorities as such, since the three ethnic groups were equal partners in the republic. He comments that:

> [the] EC offer of recognition did much to destroy this arrangement, for it put enormous pressure on the Muslims and Croats to seek independence because they did not want to live in a rump Yugoslavia . . . It is a sad comment on the ability of the EC to manage conflicts that it found comfort in this scheme simply because Yugoslavia's internal frontiers provided some kind of framework . . . What the EC disregarded was the fact that, once Yugoslavia began to break up, it was those very frontiers which fuelled war.
>
> (Zametica 1992)

The problem with Zametica's argument is that it does not recognise the importance of territoriality as the basis of claims to statehood in international society. If new states are to join the society of states, the criteria for membership is territoriality and not ethno-nationality (Jackson 1992: 8–14). As Marc Weller notes, the EC's arbitration commission applied the principle of *uti possidetis juris* in reaching its legal judgement on the right of the Yugoslav republics to self-determination. This principle developed in the context of the decolonisation process requires that self-determination must not involve changes to existing borders at the time of independence (Weller 1992: 590; Zametica 1992: 63). However, the EC's position – and that of the wider international community – that the existing inter-republican borders of Yugoslavia should become legally respected international borders was rejected by the Serbian government. It claimed that the principle of *uti possidetis* could not be applied to the internal borders of the Yugoslav state, and that any assertion of this principle amounted to interference in the internal affairs of the Yugoslav state (Weller 1992: 590). If Serbs were an equal nation with Croats and Muslims in the Yugoslav federation, why, the Serbian government asked, were Serbs living outside of Serbia only to be accorded the status of a minority under the EC's peace plan? Serbian ministers asked the EC's arbitration commission who has the right to self-determination from the standpoint of international law – a nation or a federal unit? Here, the Serbian government was arguing that if

Croats and Slovenes had a right to self-determination, Serbs living outside of Serbia had the same right to national self-determination (Zametica 1992: 63). The difficulty for the international community in reconciling these competing claims of self-determination is two-fold. First, if it legitimises the claim to self-determination of ethnic Serbs living in Croatia and Bosnia, this will challenge the principle of territoriality as the criteria of statehood in international society – placing in jeopardy the stability of borders in post-colonial international society. The international community was not according a right of self-determination to ethnic Croats and Slovenes, but to the republics of Croatia and Slovenia. Secondly, legitimising Serbian demands would send a clear signal to other ethnic groups seeking statehood that the use of force is profitable.

Nevertheless, it could be argued that the EC made a terrible blunder in recognising Croatia and Slovenia as independent in January 1992. Either recognition should have come earlier in the hope that internationalising the conflict would deter Serbia's use of force, or it should have been delayed until a lasting political settlement had been found. But the problem with the German view that Croatia and Slovenia should have been recognised in the summer of 1991 is that unless this had been accompanied by a willingness among west European governments to intervene with force to defend Croatia's territorial integrity, it is hard to see how early recognition would have stopped the fighting (Glenny 1992: 180)

FORCIBLE HUMANITARIAN INTERVENTION AND THE YUGOSLAV CRISIS

There can be no doubt that the violent dismemberment of Yugoslavia created a massive humanitarian crisis, but did this justify armed intervention to save human lives? James Gow and Jim Smith in their study of the Yugoslav crisis conclude that, 'It may be that, if not in the case of Bosnia, then in some other case in the future, the EC will find itself requiring some kind of military capability as the ultimate instrument of coercion' (Gow and Smith 1992: 55–6). The EC lacks its own defence capability, but nine of its members belong to the Western European Union (WEU) which has the potential to emerge as the defence arm of the EC. The WEU did meet in September 1991 to consider the question of sending armed escorts to back up the EC's civilian monitoring mission in Yugoslavia, but despite strong support from Germany, France and the Netherlands for sending peacekeeping forces, there was no question at this time of deploying European military forces in the absence of a durable cease-fire and a clear military and political objective (Salmon 1992: 250–2).

As the humanitarian tragedy of Bosnia unfolded through 1992[4] – with Bosnian Serb forces the worst offenders in the practice of 'ethnic cleansing', expelling hundreds of thousands of Croats and Muslims from their homes – western governments came under increasing public pressure to do more to relieve the humanitarian suffering of the civilian population. There were appeals from the Bosnian government throughout 1992 for the international community to intervene to reverse Serbia's use of force in Bosnia, with some commentators drawing parallels between Serbia's intervention in support of Bosnian Serbs and Iraq's invasion of Kuwait. If Bosnia is judged to have been invaded by another state, it has a legal right under Article 51 of the United Nations Charter to invite military assistance from other states. This right exists until the United Nations Security Council has taken steps to restore 'international peace and security', although what enforcement action the Security Council has to take before Article 51 is superseded is a matter of considerable political and legal debate.

The Security Council did place an arms embargo upon all the parties to the Yugoslav conflict. However, since the Bosnian Serb forces were better armed, and had extensive logistic support from the Milosevic government and the YPA, this strengthened them relative to the much weaker Bosnian government forces. Despite being recognised by the international community as a sovereign state, the international community was not willing through 1992 to sanction forcible intervention to restore the Bosnian government's control of its territory. Nor was it willing to create protected areas for Bosnian Muslims who were the principal victims of the Serbs' practice of 'ethnic cleansing'. The furthest that the Security Council was prepared to go was to authorise armed escorts for United Nations humanitarian relief convoys operating in Bosnia. As part of this United Nations humanitarian relief operation, British forces were deployed to Bosnia in late 1992 with a mandate to use force in self-defence. At the time of writing, it is unclear whether the Security Council's authorisation of armed escorts for humanitarian relief convoys signals the beginning of a more activist military enforcement (as against peacekeeping) role for UN forces in Bosnia.

The decision to provide armed escorts for United Nations relief convoys has been welcomed by the Bosnian government. But most international lawyers argue that in a civil war situation like the Bosnian conflict, the consent of the nominal government does not provide sufficient legality for armed intervention (see Harris 1983: 651). Instead, the Security Council has to mandate enforcement action under Chapter Seven of the United Nations Charter. Public outrage at the humanitarian suffering in Bosnia was the principal motivation behind the UN's growing military intervention, but the Security Council did not legitimise the use of force in Bosnia on humanitarian grounds. The Security Council can only legally sanction Chapter Seven enforcement action (as distinct from Chapter Six peacekeeping operations) within the borders of a sovereign state where it finds a threat to 'international peace and security'. There is nothing in the United Nations Charter, or in state practice, that otherwise permits the Security Council to legitimise intervention, since this would be in contravention of Articles 2 (4) (non-use of force except in self-defence) and 2 (7) (the non-intervention principle) of the Charter. Thus, even if western governments were to decide to escalate their military involvement in the conflict by creating, for example, protected areas for Bosnian Muslims, this would legally require additional authorisation from the United Nations Security Council.

There is a recent precedent for military intervention to create protected areas for an ethnic group under threat. In the immediate aftermath of the Gulf War, western forces intervened in northern Iraq to create 'safe havens' for the Kurdish minority. Thus, it is not surprising that attention has focused on the possibility of creating similar protected areas for those most vulnerable to 'ethnic cleansing' in Bosnia. However, it would be wrong to jump to the conclusion that the west's intervention in defence of the Kurds sets a clear precedent for humanitarian intervention in the society of states.

There was little support in the wider international community for the west's intervention in northern Iraq. The Security Council did find a threat to 'international peace and security' in the face of the massive refugee problem on the Iraq-Turkish border caused by Iraq's oppression of the Kurds, but while some commentators have pointed to the passing of Resolution 688 as indicating a new willingness in the society of states to legitimise humanitarian intervention (Chopra and Weiss, 1992), it seems that Resolution 688 was only endorsed by the Security Council because it lacked provisions for enforcement action under Articles 41 and 42 of the United Nations Charter. China most certainly, and probably the Soviet Union, would have vetoed any resolution that went beyond declaratory condemnation, fearful that this might set a precedent for future humanitarian intervention within their own internal affairs, a concern they shared with most members of the Security Council (Morris 1991: 39–42; Gardner 1991/92: 71) Thus, the claim of the western powers that Resolution 688 provided sufficient legality for their intervention in northern Iraq was greeted with considerable suspicion by other members of the Security Council, and by UN officials, fearful that the west was acting without a clear legal mandate from the Security Council (Wheeler and Morris, 1992).

Consequently, had the repression of the Kurds not taken place as a direct consequence of the war in the Gulf, it is very questionable whether the United Nations Security Council would have been prepared to pass Resolution 688, or that western governments would have intervened in the way they did (Mayall 1991: 426–9; Gardner 1991/92: 71).

Despite recognising the exceptional circumstances surrounding the western powers' creation of 'safe havens' for the Kurdish population, Richard Gardner suggests that partly as a consequence of this experience, the Security Council is:

> more likely than it was before to deal with mass repression where it can reasonably find a threat to 'international peace and security'. . . . The Council is unlikely to stand by the next time an Idi Amin or Pol Pot wages war on his own people. A massive flow of refugees across borders . . . will facilitate the finding of a 'threat to international peace and security'.
>
> (Gardner 1991/92: 72)

Yet, while it can be argued that the Security Council should legitimise United Nations military intervention where humanitarian suffering threatens wider international security, this is likely to continue to be resisted by those UN members fearful that this might set a precedent for humanitarian intervention in their internal affairs. Moreover, even if council members are prepared to find a threat to international security in the consequences of intra-state violence and mass repression, will they be prepared to support and contribute to UN enforcement action?

If the refugee problem caused by Iraq's oppression of the Kurds constituted a threat to international security, there can be no doubt that the Yugoslav conflict poses an even graver threat. The refugee problem caused by the war is on a scale not seen in Europe since 1945. At the time of writing there are grave concerns that the conflict might spill over into a wider Balkan war. Yet, while western governments have been horrified by the human suffering in the former Yugoslavia, it seems that they have decided that the costs and risks of full-scale armed intervention – of picking sides in the conflict – are not outweighed by the costs and risks of continuing with the current policy of limited intervention. It might be argued that this judgement reflects myopic self-interest on the part of western states, especially those most vulnerable to a spill-over of the conflict. Does long-term self-interest not require that western states intervene with air power and ground forces to try and limit the war, irrespective of whatever other humanitarian concerns they may feel for its victims? Full-scale intervention in Bosnia would be costly, requiring a long-term commitment to the policing of inter-communal conflicts, but it still might be prudent compared to the costs and risks of intervention if the conflict were to escalate into a regional conflagration. And if a key legitimising principle of the society of states, that is non-use of force to change existing territorial borders, is being flagrantly violated – as with the Serbs use of force in Croatia and Bosnia – there is the further question as to how far governments have a long-term security interest, whatever moral and legal obligations they may also have, in seeing that the norms and rules of international society are upheld? The problem is how do governments evaluate the all too clear costs of direct intervention in such a conflict against the possible risk that it could subsequently escalate, endangering vital security interests, or that the outcome of the conflict might be to undermine key normative principles of the society of states?

The difficulty for governments is that while in a democracy they have to respond to public opinion, they also have (as realists tell us) the protection of the security of their citizens as their first obligation. It is trying to juggle this primary responsibility against any wider moral obligations they may feel which is the appalling moral dilemma which confronts politicians who wish to define the moral community in wider terms than the national state. Robert Jackson has captured this dilemma well. I have substituted Bosnia for Somalia in his following comments as to the morality of forcible humanitarian intervention:

> Even if one could calculate in advance that on balance more lives would be saved by intervening it is still a hard choice. Such a decision cannot (and should not) avoid the question of prudence: would it be wise to intervene in [Bosnia] in circumstances of armed anarchy even if it could be justified. . . . The first duty of a statesman in such circumstances is to protect his own citizens. After that he can try and save or protect whomever else he can.
>
> (Jackson 1992: 22)

Jackson considers that governments which face a conflict of moralities have no choice but to privilege the security of their citizens over any wider moral claims. But as he hints at in the above comments, it is not certain that even on cosmopolitanist grounds, where all human lives are morally equal irrespective of national identity, armed humanitarian intervention would be justified in cases like Bosnia or Somalia. From a cosmopolitanist perspective, the question that has to be answered is will general human welfare be increased or decreased by armed intervention? The difficulty being that it is only possible in hindsight, if at all, to know whether a decision to intervene with force was the right one.

The response of west European publics to both the Kurdish and Yugoslav crises might lead to the conclusion that there is a growing sensitivity among these publics to massive human rights violations in the society of states. However, if there is a growing cosmopolitan moral awareness, at least in western states, it is worth asking why public opinion was not similarly sensitised to the terrible plight of Somalia in 1991–2, or even within the borders of CSCE Europe, to the humanitarian suffering caused by the war between Armenia and Azerbaijan in 1991–2? The answer seems to be two-fold. First, the media coverage of these other conflicts was much less intense than was the case with Bosnia, and secondly, the peoples of the former Yugoslavia are seen by west Europeans as part of European 'civilisation' in a way that the Azeris and Armenians, let alone the Somalis, are not. Indeed, the tragedy of the Yugoslav conflict for Europe is that the evils of 'ethnic cleansing' – which Europeans fervently hoped they had abolished from their culture at the end of 1945 – are scarring European civilisation once more.

Yet, awareness of the suffering of the peoples of the former Yugoslavia does not mean that western publics are prepared to pay the economic, political and ultimately, human costs of intervention to try to relieve that suffering. West European public opinion is appalled at the human suffering in Bosnia, but is it willing to risk a long and protracted commitment to the Balkans? And even if there is support among European public opinion for forcible intervention, governments have to consider how far such support would last once the human costs of intervention became clear.

CONCLUSION

In thinking about the lessons of the Yugoslav crisis, Gow and Smith concluded that:

> the principle of non-interference in a state's internal affairs may conflict with humanitarian concerns and, indeed, with a basic interest in security . . . . To prevent or manage crises and conflicts, it may be necessary to go inside borders.
>
> (Gow and Smith 1992: 52)

Although this chapter strongly affirms the importance of the linkage between the way a government treats individuals and minority groups within its borders and wider international security, the problem is that it is impossible to know whether every serious abuse of human rights or minority rights poses a threat to interstate order. Moreover, by the time an intra-state conflict has reached the point where it threatens wider security, the scope for international action to defuse the conflict may be severely limited. Thus, the logic of Gow and Smith's view is that since significant rights violations may pose a threat to interstate order, anticipatory humanitarian intervention should be legitimised on security grounds. But this raises fundamental questions as to what level of human rights and minority rights violations should trigger going inside borders, what form such intervention should take, and who is going to be willing to do this? Here, it is worth asking whether any of the three organisations under discussion here – the CSCE, EC and the United Nations Security Council – are capable of acting in such an anticipatory role?

In a sense, the logic of anticipatory intervention for reasons of both interstate security and human rights lies at the heart of the CSCE process. The problem with the CSCE is that while it has an important role to play in setting standards and monitoring compliance in the human rights field, and in de-legitimising those governments which abuse CSCE rules and principles, it is severely limited in its interventionary powers as can be seen from its response to the Yugoslav crisis. This reflects the fact that the governments of the CSCE are very jealous of their sovereign prerogatives, and very reluctant to give the CSCE the teeth to enforce its human rights rules.

In contrast to the CSCE, EC member states did demonstrate a willingness to challenge the norm of non-intervention and adopt a coercive interventionary role once the Yugoslav conflict escalated in the summer of 1991. However, had EC member states been similarly prepared to intervene in Yugoslavia's internal affairs in the months preceding the crisis, or even earlier to punish the Milosevic regime for its oppression of minority rights, it is possible that the war might have been averted, although there can be no guarantees that anticipatory intervention would have worked. If the EC is to actively go inside borders in the future as part of its crisis prevention and crisis management roles, this is likely to be most effective if it can be pursued in concert with the US and other G7 (Group of Seven) partners.

But what principles should guide the EC and the wider international community in dealing with intra-state conflicts in post-Cold War Europe? Does a choice have to be made between the rights of states and the principle of territorial integrity, and the rights of individuals and groups within the state? In the Yugoslav case, the initial aim of keeping Yugoslavia together was based on the hope that these two principles could be reconciled, as well as a fear of the consequences of being seen to legitimise secession in the society of states. The Yugoslav conflict demonstrates the difficulties of dealing with the conflict between demands for national self-determination on the one hand, and respect for existing borders on the other. The international community is determined in managing the break-up of Yugoslavia that territoriality and not ethno-nationality will determine claims to sovereign statehood. But while no legitimacy will be afforded by international society to Serbian territorial conquests achieved through the use of force, the *de facto* situation on the ground in Bosnia at the time of writing is that superior force has triumphed. But if the Serbs are seen to have got away with their 'ethnic cleansing' and re-drawing of existing borders through the use of force, this will set a very dangerous precedent for post-Cold War Europe.

EC member states through their economic and political muscle can help to strengthen the protection of human rights and minority rights in post-Cold War Europe, but the hardest question that the Yugoslav crisis raises for EC member states is what do they do if political and economic instruments fail to prevent gross violations of human rights and minority rights? EC member states have the military capability to forcibly intervene in the Yugoslav crisis – although it is very unlikely that they would do so without United States backing – but at the time of writing, it seems that western states have made the judgement that the costs of armed intervention to protect human lives are significantly higher than the costs of the existing policy of limited intervention. Put differently, the humanitarian impulse to intervene is not joined by a strong enough sense that this is also necessary on security grounds, and that there are clear political and military objectives which would warrant this type of intervention. But if western governments should come to decide that forcible intervention in Bosnia is justified – for reasons of both national self-interest and moral obligation – this legally will require authorisation from the United Nations Security Council.

The Security Council can mandate states or regional bodies to undertake enforcement action on its behalf under Chapter Eight of the United Nations Charter, but it will only authorise enforcement action within the borders of a sovereign state if it finds a threat to 'international peace and security'. International society is not sufficiently solidarist on ideas of justice to legitimise a duty of collective humanitarian intervention. And even if general principles could be arrived at for deciding when humanitarian intervention was permissible – there is always the realist assertion that states will abuse these principles – applying them selectively depending upon considerations of national self-interest. Additionally, the refusal of the Security Council to lend legitimacy to the west's use of force to protect the Kurds in northern Iraq in 1991 suggests that the Council will be very unwilling to mandate the use of force inside state borders if this is seen as setting a precedent for humanitarian intervention in the internal affairs of UN member states.

Against this, western dominance of the Security Council at the end of the Cold War – and the growing incidence of intra-state conflict in post-Cold War international society – is leading Council members to increasingly accept, however reluctantly, that a state's behaviour towards its own people can have consequences for wider international security. But even if the Security Council is willing in the future to cross the rubicon on forcible intervention inside state borders, by the time an intra-state conflict has escalated to the point where there is agreement in the Council that it does pose a major threat to international security, the scope for United Nations interventionary action is likely to be extremely limited.

Although forcible intervention is the ultimate sanction, it would be wrong to exaggerate the utility of force in dealing with humanitarian crises like the Yugoslav conflict. The society of states through organisations like the CSCE, the EC and the United Nations can seek to mediate between the warring factions, and provide peacekeeping forces where the parties agree, but where this is unsuccessful, it is doubtful that forcible intervention can produce a lasting political settlement. Indeed, there may be cases where this is counter-productive – leading to a greater loss of life than a policy of non-intervention. Against this, if political and economic means of inter-vention exercised by individual states – or ideally by the wider international community – fail to stop violent conflict and massive violations of human rights, any final settlement will be determined by the balance of military forces on the ground. In the case of Bosnia, the imposition of the arms embargo – in the hope that this would reduce the intensity of human suffering – has effectively denied the Bosnian government the right to individual and collective self-defence. Forcible intervention does mean picking sides, and it must always be guided by prudential considerations (be they realist or cosmopolitanist), but is it not justified if it is the only means left to stop massive human suffering? These are extremely difficult questions for governments and publics to answer, and they bring us back to the real lesson of the Yugoslav conflict for post-Cold War Europe: the importance of building through the CSCE – but especially the EC – a system of crisis prevention, and one which would be based on recognition of the linkages between human rights and international security.

ACKNOWLEDGEMENTS

The author wishes to express his considerable thanks to Robert Jackson,

Ken Booth, James Gow and Justin Morris for their comments on earlier drafts of this chapter.

NOTES

1 For reasons of space, this chapter will not discuss the importance of the Council of Europe in protecting human rights, although it is recognised that the Council has a role to play in fostering closer links with the CSCE, perhaps through the machinery of the European Court of Human Rights.
2 Stephen Larrabee has argued that to increase its effectiveness in future, the CSCE may require a system of qualified majority voting and 'formidable enforcement capabilities at its disposal' (Larrabee 1992: 46). The idea of the North Atlantic Treaty Organisation (NATO) becoming the enforcement arm of the CSCE has not met with an enthusiastic response. NATO has been prepared to accept the possibility of contributing forces for CSCE peacekeeping operations, but only if such forces could be deployed with the consent of the warring parties, and only if all 52 CSCE members agreed.
3 Some international lawyers do question how far it might be legitimate for EC member states to employ economic coercion against another state without the consent of the United Nations Security Council. It is argued that sanctions constitute a violation of Article 2 (4) (non-use of force) and 2 (7) (non-intervention) of the United Nations Charter, and therefore only have legitimacy if mandated by the Security Council under Chapter Seven of the United Nations Charter (See Harris 1983: 641).
4 Pressure from public opinion led the governments of the United States, Britain, France and Belgium to seek a Security Council Resolution (passed unanimously under Chapter Seven of the United Nations Charter) in May 1992, placing mandatory economic sanctions upon Serbia, in the hope that it would cease its use of force in Bosnia.

Chapter 9

Conclusion
G. Wyn Rees

This book has attempted to sketch out the likely issues that will dominate Europe in the post-Cold War era. It has focused upon four issues of security, economic development, the environment and human rights and it has sought to explain the variety of levels on which these issues, and the problems that result from them, must be analysed and understood.

The purpose of this concluding chapter is threefold. First, it will seek to demonstrate that all the issues discussed by their respective authors in Part II are interrelated and need to be studied in parallel with one another. Secondly, it will argue that although the issues are pan-European, the resulting problems vary between the two halves of the continent. Finally, it will be contended that the solutions to these problems will also differ between east and west and will, to a large extent, depend upon what vision of Europe is decided upon by its member states.

INTERLINKING ISSUES

For the purposes of clarity, the four issue areas in this book were analysed separately. Yet it is clear from each of the chapters that the issues do not exist in isolation, but rather overlap with each other. It is in fact artificial to separate them out for they are intimately connected. As the continent as a whole becomes increasingly interdependent, so do the issues and problems facing the countries that are a part of the region.

The security agenda, as McInnes has shown, is now both harder to define and no longer just state-centred. It is a broadened agenda that encapsulates a range of risks, rather than overt threats, that largely escaped attention during the Cold War. It is more concerned with the continent as a whole because it is recognised that conflict and instability in one corner of Europe may have widespread ramifications for all the rest. An example of this has been the war in former Yugoslavia, which has drawn in all the major organisations that have European membership, such as the Economic Community (EC), the North Atlantic Treaty Organisation (NATO), the Western European Union (WEU), and the Conference on Security and Cooperation in Europe (CSCE), and has resulted in a tide of refugees crossing into neighbouring countries. As the threat of large-scale interstate war has receded, attention has switched to the level of individuals and groups of people, in order to address the question of what makes people feel 'insecure'. At one end of the spectrum this still includes the threat of conflict – particularly for people caught up in civil wars – but at the other end of the spectrum it involves such matters as the perceived quality of life, linking it to environmental and human rights issues.

The economic agenda can be seen clearly to link with the other issues. The political and demographic stability of societies in Europe, notably in the east, is increasingly dependent upon the ability of governments to deliver a satisfactory standard of living for their people. Through the medium of modern communications, and due to the greater openness of eastern societies, people from all over the continent are conscious of the levels of income in the richest states of western Europe. In this way, there is a linkage between economic issues and security on the one hand, and the economic rights of an individual on the other. Even states that enjoy a high standard of living cannot isolate themselves from the economic problems of those around them.

If rising expectations of people in the poorer parts of the continent are not assuaged then there is a danger of civil unrest and the outbreak of violent protest. This could lead to the overthrow of governments and the accession to power of hardline leaders, possibly with the support of their security establishments or with the ability to mobilise nationalist feeling. The implication for surrounding countries is that they might be faced with one of two scenarios. Either they might have to contend with aggressive behaviour from this neighbour as its leadership seeks to employ its foreign policy as a means of diverting attention from internal problems. Alternatively, economic chaos could result in a large-scale movement of economic migrants. For countries watching a crisis develop in a nearby state, they would have to weigh carefully whether their interests would be better served by providing economic aid to prevent economic breakdown from occurring in the first place, or attempting to avoid involvement. In the case of EC members, the problem has been intensified by the progress towards the abolition of border controls which might ease the problem for migrants in moving from east to west.

Environmental questions are also interdependent with other issues. Spear discussed the manner in which the environment is related to economic and to security issues. It is linked to economic issues in terms of the level of economic development that has generated environmental degradation as well as in the type and scale of damage that has been incurred. Related to this is the economic cost of rectifying the damage and the ability of the polluter to pay these costs. On the other hand, the threat of an ecological catastrophe has obvious implications for security across the continent. It has long been appreciated that damage to the environment, such as chemicals in rivers or acid rain, pays no heed to state boundaries. Therefore there is a need to address the concerns of poorer neighbouring states as well as putting one's own house in order. Such an example of this is the debate surrounding the provision of western aid to east European countries to modify some of their nuclear power stations which are of flawed design.

Wheeler has demonstrated that human rights are also to be linked with security and economic issues. Human rights raise the question of to what extent the individual should have the right to be free from threat, be it from the state he/she lives within or from external aggression. This links in with the wider question as to what responsibility governments should bear for protecting individuals in neighbouring states from the abuse of their rights. Secondly, human rights is an economic issue to the extent that individuals may choose to migrate to another part of Europe if they feel that their state is not meeting their expectations as consumers. The problem of immigration and the pressure it places upon host states to cope with the inflow of people, promises to loom ever larger in Europe in the future.

COMMON ISSUES, DIFFERENT PROBLEMS

A central tenet of the book has been that the continent is becoming more interdependent as the last vestiges of Cold War wither away. As a consequence of this, the four issues that were analysed in Part II are argued to be applicable to Europe as a whole. However, as each of the chapters reveals, the issues manifest themselves as different problems in the two halves of Europe. This can either be in terms of the nature, or the intensity, of the problems. This is hardly to be found surprising considering that the imposition of the Cold War ensured that the two halves of the continent developed separately from one another for over forty years. It does mean that although the issues of security, economic development, the environment and human rights are relevant to Europe as a whole; attempts to remedy the problems resulting from these issues will require an understanding of the differences between eastern and western Europe.

In eastern Europe there is great diversity between the states in the region in respect to their geographical size and resources, their political maturity and stability and their levels of economic development. The northern tier states of Poland, Hungary and the former Czechoslovakia – previously the backbone of the Warsaw Pact – are economically more advanced than their southern neighbours. States such as Albania and Bulgaria are much weaker, reflecting the neglect and paralysis of their post-war governments and a long history of under-development. This diversity will result in varying abilities between states in eastern Europe to resolve their difficulties. However, what all states in the region have in common is their desire to undertake modernisation programmes that will move them away from the straightjackets of command economies. These are being promoted at varying speeds whilst simultaneously experimenting with democratic forms of government.

All four issues manifest themselves as chronic problems in eastern Europe. First of all there is a security vacuum in the region at the very time when the removal of Soviet control has allowed long-suppressed territorial disputes and ethnic rivalries to rise to the surface. Secondly, there is economic turmoil as countries seek to lay the foundations of market economies amidst declining industrial output, crushing debt and increasing levels of unemployment and inflation. Thirdly, countries are now having to face up to several decades of environmental damage and neglect, with all its implications for public health and the reorientation of east European heavy industry. Finally, with the instability in the region, human rights are under threat or, in some of the worst cases such as Croatia and Bosnia, openly abused.

One of the key difficulties for the states of eastern Europe is that they lack membership of important international institutions. Some of these institutions, such as the EC or NATO, could provide them with secure frameworks and the material assistance from which to tackle their problems. Unfortunately, their former institutions collapsed with the ending of the Cold War. As a group of states experiencing similar problems, the east Europeans see little prospect of forming new institutions themselves due to their collective weakness. Not only do many states, such as Poland and the fragmented Czechoslovakia, mistrust each other; they are also uneasy about the dominant role that the Russian Federation might play in any new structures. Instead they look to the west to provide them with aid and membership of western institutions.

In contrast, west European states are not in such a position of weakness as their eastern counterparts. The problems they face are different in nature, and the priority they would attach to the four issues would be at variance with those of the east. Their societies are generally stable and their security structures have survived the rigours of the Cold War. The success of their market economies are evident in their high levels of productivity and standards of living. Yet the very success of west European economies has brought with it greater interdependency and sensitivity to the policies of their neighbours, through such indicators as interest rates and currency fluctuations. It has also led to a larger debate about the future extent of integration in the west, that was discussed in Chapter 6.

The more difficult and pressing question for west European leaders lies not in dealing with their own problems, numerous though they are, but in determining how best to respond to the demands of the east. Recognising that the continent is interdependent implies that they cannot ignore the difficulties in the other half of the continent; for reasons of morality as well as self-interest. Economic chaos, civil wars and environmental disasters in the east might all have grave implications for states in the west in the form of mass migrations, refugees and pollution. The institutional frameworks that offer the greatest potential benefit to the east are the EC, NATO and the CSCE. Of these, the former two are exclusively western organisations, whilst the latter has always enjoyed a membership across and outside the continent. Although these institutions were developed in a different era, they are now being called upon to adapt to the needs of the new situation in Europe.

Western states are justifiably cautious of taking on the burden for the security and economic regeneration of eastern Europe. Should all states be helped or only those who have attained a specified level of economic development or display democratic credentials? This might lead to assistance being given to countries like Poland and Hungary but not to Romania. There is already pressure from within the EC to shift resources from the richer northern to the poorer southern states, through the 'cohesion' programme and taking on an additional assistance effort in eastern Europe would place enormous strains upon western economies. Germany, despite possessing the strongest economy in Europe, has struggled under the weight of rebuilding the former German Democratic Republic and assisting neighbouring states in the east. As for extending security guarantees to the east, this would threaten to embroil western countries in future conflicts not of their own making and from which they would find it difficult to extricate themselves.

However, responding to the desire of eastern countries to join western organisations raises a deeper question. It demands from west European countries a clear vision not only of how they see the future of their own states, but what future they envisage for the continent as a whole. There is a need here for what former President Bush called the 'vision thing'; to define the sort of Europe they seek to work towards and to integrate eastern countries into that programme. This raises the question to what extent western solutions are appropriate in eastern Europe and what will be the cost to the west of diluting their institutions in order to admit their ailing eastern brethren?

COMPETING VISIONS AND CONTESTED FRAMEWORKS

To ask whether the west is prepared or capable of resolving the problems of the whole continent, is to open a Pandora's box of uncertainties. A system level framework is required to meet the needs of the east, but a major obstacle is proving to be the disagreement between western states over their visions of the future of Europe. There does not appear to be a consensus in the first place over which frameworks should be developed to satisfy the needs of western states: quite apart from the question of whether and when to allow eastern states to join them. It is recognised that the admission of a host of east European states, with their own complex array of problems, would inevitably have a major impact upon the way in which those frameworks subsequently developed.

Although no single framework could provide comprehensive solutions to all the problems, the EC is the structure of foremost interest to east European regimes. Recognition of this fact was demonstrated by the granting of associate membership of the EC to Poland, Hungary and former Czechoslovakia in November 1991. The Community has the broadest areas of competence, spreading, through the process of political union, from economic affairs into foreign policy and security matters. Thus, membership of the EC could confer a host of benefits on eastern governments; including economic aid, access to the huge internal market, technological know-how and financial provision to deal with environmental problems. The expansion of Community interest into foreign and security policy, as shown by the negotiations surrounding the Maastricht Summit of December 1991, would also prove attractive to east European countries.

But a consensus has still to emerge in the west over the question of how the European Community is to develop. Further economic integration and the additional pursuit of political union has proved to be a divisive question amongst the twelve – as illustrated by the rejection of the Maastricht Treaty in the Danish referendum of June 1992 (*The Economist* 1992). When looking at the enlargement of the Community, two broad schools of thought can be discerned. The first, spearheaded by France and the European Commission, wishes to see a deepening of the process of integration within the west before membership is offered to countries in the east. Even then, entry would only be permitted when a substantial degree of convergence had been attained and strict criteria had been fulfilled. The fear expressed by proponents of this approach is that the forward movement of the Community would be derailed by inclusion of east European states that would bring problems of such a magnitude as to absorb all the energies of the Community for the foreseeable future. They express the anxiety that the EC would become so bloated with new members that it would be incapable of efficient decision-making.

An opposing school of thought, epitomised by Britain, contends that the Community should be prepared to sacrifice deepening in the short to medium term, in order to facilitate the widening to embrace new members. This view is championed by states that feel uneasy about the shift of the Community from progression towards a single economic market into a march towards political integration. It argues that to delay the entry of east European members would be a mistake for their needs are too pressing to ignore. Proponents of early membership argue that something has to be done quickly to avert the threat of enfeebled eastern economies sliding into chaos, with all the attendant risks for the wider region. Although it is acknowledged that European Free Trade Area (EFTA) states, such as Sweden, have a prior claim to entry, this should not stand in the way of east European membership. On current expectations, the earliest that east European states could hope to enter the EC would be the end of the decade.

An attempt to bridge the divide between these two opposing views was endorsed by the Commission President, Jacques Delors, who advocated a policy conceived around the idea of concentric circles. Within these circles, states in various stages of economic development would reside in differing levels of association with the core members of the Community. States closer to the core would therefore not be held back from progress towards integration by members in outer circles, who might be relatively economically backward. To some this smacks of the 'Finlandization' of the east and raises the deeper question of how appropriate western dictated solutions would be to eastern problems. There is clearly a danger that countries in the east, far removed from Brussels, could find themselves the victims of a type of core-periphery model with the Community. They might develop into economic backwaters where substandard goods would be dumped by the richer members and whose problems, such as environmental decay, would be ignored.

NATO is the second framework to which eastern states are eager to acquire membership. Although the Alliance suffers from being an organisation associated with the military confrontation of the Cold War, it has much to commend it in the eyes of the east. This is because it represents stability and the sort of military guarantees that eastern states believe to be vital for their long-term security. Furthermore, the Alliance has struggled to adapt itself to the new European situation in which it finds itself. At the London and Rome Summits, of July 1990 and November 1991 respectively, it has sought to broaden its area of competence, by signalling that economic and environmental issues are legitimate areas for its concern. In these ways it has made itself more relevant to the needs and concerns of states in both halves of the continent.

Yet, similar to the competing visions of the EC, there is a debate over the future development of the Alliance. The debate concentrates upon the extent of its adaptability; whether its trans-Atlantic focus is still appropriate or whether the Alliance should be superseded by specifically European institutions. The Western European Union has been mooted as an institution that could fulfil this role, linked to a European Community that had a major role in foreign and defence policy. Proponents of this approach are led by France, which although not calling for the end of NATO, has argued that its importance should decline. Opponents of this view, such as Britain, have argued for the continuing centrality of NATO in order to allow the US to continue to play a major role on the continent.

Resolving this debate about the future development of the Alliance would have to precede the entry of new members. But the prospect of allowing in states from the east causes considerable disquiet among existing members. A host of new states would undoubtedly make decision-making within the Alliance more problematical, assuming that majority voting was not introduced. Secondly, is the added security concerns that would result from the membership of eastern states. The present members of NATO are fearful of becoming entangled in a series of disputes in east Europe, over such matters as disputed borders and ethnic tensions, that simmered for a long time beneath the apparently calm surface of the Cold War. Extending Article Five of the NATO Treaty, which regards an attack upon one member as an attack upon all (NATO 1981), into the east would open up the prospect of western troops being called upon to die in obscure conflicts.

Whilst NATO members fear the instability that could result from the overspill of eastern conflicts and endorse the concept of including eastern states in western institutions, they are unwilling to become responsible for resolving the problems of their former adversaries. A sop has been found in the form of a consultative body, the North Atlantic Cooperation Council, but the best that east European states can hope for in the future is some type of associational status that falls short of real membership. Once membership is offered to one of these states, there is an inescapable logic that will demand that every state be permitted to join the club. This logic holds true for both NATO and the EC.

The last framework of significance, the CSCE, is in a different position to the EC and NATO because eastern states already are members. From its stable membership during the Cold War of thirty-five, the CSCE has now expanded to include fifty-two states (Serbia having been suspended). Nevertheless, it shares with the former two organisations a confusion about its future importance and the role that it can play in assisting east European states with their difficulties.

The attraction of the CSCE to east European states lies in its pan-European legitimacy: they are not outcasts knocking at the door of their richer neighbours. It has played a constructive part in ratifying the changes in post-Cold War Europe – such as the Conventional Forces in Europe Treaty (CFE) and the unification of Germany – and has provided a forum for discussion between the two halves of the continent. The CSCE has also seen its status increase due, as Wheeler has described, to its role in seeking to end the conflict in former Yugoslavia. In these ways it offers eastern states an evolving security framework and avoids the impression that western solutions are being imposed upon east European countries. With the CSCE's remit extending from security and human rights issues to the environment, there appears much that is attractive in this institution for the future.

However, the muscle that lies behind the rhetoric of the CSCE is still limited. The United States has been sceptical about its security value and the organisation has little power in the field of assisting eastern states economically. Western states remain cautious about placing too much reliance on the CSCE for they regard its size as unwieldy and its members, interests too diverse. There is still a perception that the CSCE is a talking shop. Hence there is doubt as to whether it could prove to be an effective security framework for the continent and a belief that it would need to defer in crises to organisations comprising smaller numbers of more homogenous states.

Thus there does not appear to be a consensus either on the sort of Europe that the west will seek to engineer, nor on which framework will provide the vehicle for integrating the east. Such confusion precludes any serious discussion of whether western solutions are the most appropriate for eastern problems – an issue highlighted by both Croft and Spear. By default a policy of 'wait and see' seems to have emerged. The most likely result is that no single framework will be adopted, rather overlapping circles will be preserved in which institutions maintain selected areas of competence (Hyde-Price 1991).

EUROPE AND THE WIDER WORLD

With the end of the Cold War, Europe now presents a clearer identity to the rest of the world. In the past it was a region within a global superpower competition but that status, as well as the competition itself, has now concluded. There is a growing expectation that Europe will want to play a larger role in world affairs and exercise influence commensurate with its size and power. Evidence of this desire has been forthcoming in a number of areas. In trade, for example, there has been an unwillingness to see west European interests sacrificed at the Uruguay Round of the General Agreement on Trade and Tariffs (GATT) negotiations, even at the expense of incurring hostility from the United States. In environmental matters, the EC exercised a high profile at the Earth Summit in Rio in June 1992. In security affairs, the Community, reluctantly but with prompting from the United States, has sought to take the lead in restoring peace in the Balkans under the leadership of Lord Carrington and subsequently Lord Owen. In these and many other ways, Europe seems to be seizing the opportunity to determine its own destiny.

Yet to a great extent, the role that Europe will play in the world will be determined by the approach adopted to the four issue areas that have been investigated in this book. For the manner in which these issues are addressed and the effectiveness of dealing with the problems will help to define Europe's identity. They may also come to act in the future as models for the rest of the world. The issues of security, economics, environment and human rights play a vital part in determining the strength of Europe, its degree of integration and its level of stability. Failure to address these issues effectively, across the continent as a whole, is likely to result in a Europe focusing inward, preoccupied with periodic conflicts and internal turmoil (Mearsheimer 1990). Success in meeting the challenges of these issues will demand considerable effort but offers the prospect of an outward-looking Europe, able to engage constructively in world affairs.

Bibliography

Anderson, J. (1986) *The Rise of the Modern State*, Brighton: Wheatsheaf Books.

Barnes, I. with Preston, J. (1988) *The European Community*, London: Longman.

Barry Jones, R. J. (1986) *Conflict and Control in the World Economy: Contemporary Economic Realism and Neo-mercantilism*, Brighton: Wheatsheaf Books.

Barry Jones, R. J. (ed.) (1988) *The Worlds of Political Economy: Alternative Approaches to the Study of Contemporary Political Economy*, London: Pinter Publishers.

Barry Jones, R. J. and Willetts, P. (eds) (1984) *Interdependence on Trial: Studies in the Theory and Reality of Contemporary Interdependence*, London: Pinter Publishers.

Baylis, J. (1992) 'The evolution of NATO strategy, 1949–90', in C. McInnes (ed.) *Security and Strategy in the New Europe*, London: Routledge.

Beddington-Behrens, E. (1966) *Is There Any Choice? Britain Must Join Europe*, Harmondsworth: Penguin Books.

Bergner, J. (1991) *The New Superpowers: Germany, Japan, the US, and the New World Order*, New York: St Martins Press.

Birch, J. (1990) *The New Eastern Europe and the Question of European Unity*, Sheffield Papers in International Studies, no. 4, Sheffield University, Department of Politics.

Birnbaum, K., Binter, J. and Badzik, S. (eds) (1991) *Towards a Future European Peace Order?*, London: Macmillan.

Booth, K. (1987) 'Nuclear deterrence and "World War Three": how will history judge?', in R. Kolkowicz (ed.) *The Logic of Nuclear Terror*, London: Allen and Unwin.

Booth, K. (1990) 'Steps towards a stable peace in Europe: a theory and practice of coexistence', *International Affairs*, 66, 1, 17–46.

Bowker, M. and Williams, P. (1988) *Superpower Détente: A Reappraisal*, London, Sage for the Royal Institute of International Affairs.

Brett, E. (1985) *The World Economy Since the War: The Politics of Uneven Development*, London: Macmillan.

Brodie, B. (1946) *The Absolute Weapon*, New York: Harcourt Brace.

Brown, L. (1986) 'Redefining national security', in L. Brown et al., *State of the World 1986: A Worldwatch Institute Report on Progress Towards a Sustainable Society*, New York: Norton.

Brown, N. (1989) 'Climate ecology and international security', *Survival*, 31, 6, 519–32.

Bull, H. (1977) *The Anarchical Society*, London: Macmillan.

Buzan, B. (1983) *People, States and Fear: The National Security Problem in International Relations*, London: Harvester Wheatsheaf.

Buzan, B. (1991) *People, States and Fear: An Agenda for International Security Studies in the Post-Cold War Era*, 2nd edn, London: Harvester Wheatsheaf.

Buzan, B., Kelstrup, M., Lemaitre, P., Tromer, E. and Waever, O. (1990) *The European Security Order Recast: Scenarios for the Post-Cold War Era*, London: Pinter Press.

Calleo, D. (1989) 'NATO and some lessons of history', in J. Golden et al. (eds) *NATO at Forty: Change, Continuity and Prospects*, London: Westview.

Calleo, D. and Rowland, B. (1973) *America and The World Political Economy*, Bloomington: Indiana University Press.

Carter, N. (1992) 'The greening of Labour', in M. Smith and J. Spear (eds) *The Changing Labour Party*, London: Routledge.

Carter, N. (1992a) 'British politics and the environment', in W. Wale (ed.) *Developments in Politics 3*, Ormskirk: Causeway Press.

Cartwright, J. (1989) 'Conserving nature, decreasing debt', *Third World Quarterly*, 11, 114–27.

Chopra, J. and Weiss, T. (1992) 'Sovereignty is no longer sacrosanct: codifying humanitarian intervention', *Ethics and International Affairs*, 6, 95–117.

Clark, I. (1989) *The Hierarchy of States*, Cambridge: Cambridge University Press.

Coffey, P. (1988) *Main Economic Areas of the EEC – Towards 1992*, Dordercht: Kluwer.

Conradt, D. (1989) *The German Polity*, 4th edn, London: Longman.

Cox, M. (1986) 'The cold war system', *Critique*, 17, 17–82.

Croft, S. (1992) 'NATO and nuclear strategy', in C. McInnes (ed.) *Security and Strategy in the New Europe*, London: Routledge.

Cviic, C. (1991) *Remaking the Balkans*, London: Pinter Press.

Cviic, C. (1992) 'Implications of the crisis in south-eastern Europe', in New Dimensions of International Security, Part 1, *Adelphi Papers*, no. 265, IISS, 282–92.

Dahlberg, K., Soros, M., Feraru, A., Harf, J. and Trout, B. (1985) *Environment and the Global Arena: Actors, Values, Policies and Futures*, Durham: Duke University Press.

DePorte, A. (1979) *Europe Between the Superpowers*, London: Yale University Press.

De Tocqueville, Alexis (1863) *Democracy in America*, 2nd edn, trans. H. Reeve, Cambridge, Sever and Francis.

Deudney, D. (1991) 'Environment and security: muddled thinking', *Bulletin of the Atomic Scientists*, 47, part 3.

Deudney, D. (1992) 'The mirage of eco-war: the weak relationship among global environmental change, national security and interstate violence', in I. Rowlands and M. Green (eds) *Global Environmental Change and International Relations*, Basingstoke: Macmillan, in association with Millennium, *Journal of International Studies*.

Dosser, D. Gowland, D. and Hartley, K. (1982) *Collaboration of Nations: A Study of European Economic Policy*, Oxford: Martin Robertson.

Durning, A. (1991) 'Asking how much is enough?', in *State of the World 1991: A Worldwatch Institute Report on Progress Towards a Sustainable Society*, London: Norton.

Ecoglasnost, (1991) 'The rise of the ecology movement in Bulgaria', in S. Parkin (ed.) *Green Light on Europe*, London: Heretic Books.

Economides, S. (1992) *The Balkan Agenda: Security and Regionalism in the New Europe*, London Defence Papers 10, Published by Brassey's for the Centre for Defence Studies.

Economist, The (1992) Yearbook 1991, London: Economist Books.

Edwards, C. (1985) *The Fragmented World: Competing Perspectives on Trade, Money and Crisis*, London: Methuen.

Elkington, J. and Burke, T. (1987) *The Green Capitalists: Industry's Search for Environmental Excellence*, London: Gollancz.

Elkington, J. and Hailes, J. (1990) *Green Consumer Guide: From Shampoo to Champagne, How to Buy Goods That Don't Cost the Earth*, London: Gollancz.

Elster, J. (1990) 'Marxism and methodological individualism', in P. Birnbaum and J. Leca (eds) *Individualism*, Oxford: Clarendon.

Foot, P. (1992) 'The end of Eurocentrism and its consequences', in C. McInnes (ed.) *Security and Strategy in the New Europe*, London: Routledge.

Franck, T. and Rodley, N. (1973) 'After Bangladesh: the law of humanitarian intervention by force', *American Journal International Law*, 67, 275–305.

Freedman, L. (1989) *The Evolution of Nuclear Strategy*, 2nd edn, London: Macmillan.

Freedman, L. and Gow, J. (1992) 'Humanitarian intervention: the case of Yugoslavia', in *To Loosen the Bonds of Wickedness*, London: Brassey's.

French, H. (1991) 'Restoring the east European and Soviet environments', in *State of the World 1991: A Worldwatch Institute Report on Progress Towards a Sustainable Society*, London: Norton.

Fritzsche, H. (1989) 'The security debate in the Evangelical Church of the GDR', in O. Waever, P. Lemaitre and G. Tromer (eds) *European Polyphony: Perspectives Beyond East–West Confrontation*, London: Macmillan.

Frohlich, N. and Oppenheimer, J. (1978) *Modern Political Economy*, Englewood Cliffs, NJ: Prentice-Hall.

Fukuyama, F. (1989) 'The end of history', *National Interest*, no.16.

Fukuyama, F. (1992) 'Democratisation and international security', in New Dimensions of International Security Part 2, *Adelphi Papers*, no. 266, IISS, 1424

Gardner, R. (1991/92) 'International law and the use of force: Paper 11', in New Dimensions of International Security Part 2, *Adelphi Papers*, no. 266, IISS, 64–73.

Geddes, A. (1988) '1992 and the environment – sovereignty well lost?', *New Law Journal*, 138, 826–8.

George, S. (1990) 'Managing the global house: redefining economics', in C. Hartman and P. Vilanova (eds) *Paradigms Lost: The Post Cold War Era*, London: Pluto Press.

George, S. (1990a) *The European Community: A Structuralist Perspective*, Sheffield Papers in International Studies, no. 5, University of Sheffield, Department of Politics.

George, S. (1991) *Politics and Policy in the European Community*, 2nd edn, Oxford: Oxford University Press.

Gerle, E. (1989) 'From anti-nuclearism to a new détente in the 1980s', in M. Kaldor, G. Holden and R. Falk (eds) *The New Détente: Rethinking East–West Relations*, London: Verso.

Gill, S. and Law, D. (1988) *The Global Political Economy*, Brighton: Harvester Wheatsheaf.

Gillespie, R. (1990) 'The break-up of the socialist family: party-union relations in Spain, 1982–9', *West European Politics*, 13, 1, 47–63.

Gillette, P. and Frank, W. (1990) *The Sources of Soviet Naval Conduct*, Lexington: Lexington, D. C. Heath.

Gilpin, R. (1987) *The Political Economy of International Relations*, Princeton: Princeton University Press.

Gladwyn, Lord (1966) *The European Idea*, London: Weidenfeld and Nicolson.

Glazer, N. (1978) 'Individual rights against group rights', in E. Kamenka and A. Erh-Soon Tay (eds) *Human Rights*, London: Edward Arnold.

Gleick, P. (1991) 'Environment and security: the clear connections', *Bulletin of the Atomic Scientists*. 47, part 3.

Glenny, Misha (1992) *The Killing of Yugoslavia: Yugoslavia at War*, London: Penguin Books.

Gnesotto, N. (1992) 'European union after Minsk and Maastricht', *International Affairs*, 68, 2, 223–32.

Gorbachev, M. (1988) *Perestroika: New Thinking for Our Country and the World*, updated edn, London: Fontana.

Gore, A. (1992) *Earth in the Balance: Forging a New Common Purpose*, London: Earthscan Publications.

Gow, J. (1991) 'Deconstructing Yugoslavia', *Survival*, 33, 4, 291–312.

Gow, J. (1992) *Legitimacy and the Military: The Yugoslav Crisis*, London: Belhaven Press.

Gow, J. and Smith, J. (1992) *Peace-Making, Peace-Keeping: European Security and the Yugoslav Wars*, London Defence Papers 11, Published by Brassey's for the Centre for Defence Studies.

Gray, C. (1982) *Strategic Studies and Public Policy*, Lexington: University of Kentucky Press.

Groom, A. and Taylor, P. (1975) *Functionalism: Theory and Practice in International Relations*, London: University of London Press.

Grubb, M. (1990) 'The greenhouse effect: negotiating targets', *International Affairs* 66, 1, 67–89.

Haas, P. (1992) 'Obtaining international environmental protection through epistemic consensus', in I. Rowlands and M. Greene (eds) *Global Environmental Change and International Relations*, Basingstoke: Macmillan, in association with Millennium, *Journal of International Studies*.

Hall, J. (1985) *Powers and Liberties: The Causes and Consequences of the Rise of the West*, Oxford: Basil Blackwell.

Halliday, F. (1986) *The Making of the Second Cold War*, 2nd Edn, London: Verso.

Halliday, F. (1990) 'Nationalism is not necessarily the path to a free world', *New Statesman and Society*, 30 March.

Hardin, G. (1968) 'The tragedy of the Commons', *Science*, 162, 1243–8.

Harris, D. (1983) *Cases and Materials on International Law*, 3rd edn, London: Sweet and Maxwell.

Harrop, J. (1989) *The Political Economy of European Integration*, Aldershot: Edward Elgar.

Havel, V. (1991) 'The power of the powerless', in *Without Force or Lies*, San Francisco: Mercury; originally published by Unwin Hyman, London.

Hayek, F. (1973) *Law, Legislation and Liberty: Rules and Order, Vol.1*, London: Routledge and Kegan Paul.

Hayek, F. (1976) *Law, Legislation and Liberty: The Mirage of Social Justice, Vol.2*, London: Routledge and Kegan Paul.

Hoffmann, S. (1965) *The State of War: Essays on the Theory and Practice of International Relations*, New York: Praeger.

Holdgate, M., Kaffas, M. and White, G. (eds) (1982) *The World Environment 1972–1982*, Dublin: United Nations Environmental Programme, Tycooly International Publishing.

Holland, S. (1980) *Uncommon Market: Capital, Class and Power in the European Community*, London: Macmillan.

Holsti, K. (1983) *International Politics: A Framework for Analysis*, 4th edn, Engelwood Cliffs, NJ: Prentice-Hall.

Howard, M. (1976) *War in European History*, Oxford: Oxford University Press.

Hyde-Price, A. (1991) 'East central Europe in the 1990s', *Arms Control: Contemporary Security Policy*, 12, 2, 250–2.

Hyde-Price, A. (1991) *European Security Beyond the Cold War: Four Scenarios for the Year 2010*, London: Sage.

IISS (1992) *Strategic Survey 1991–92*, London: Brassey's for the International Institute for Strategic Studies.

Jachtenfuchs, M. (1990) 'The European Community and the protection of the ozone layer', *Journal of Common Market Studies*, 28, 3, 261–77.

Jay, D. (1968) *After the Common Market: A Better Alternative for Britain*, Harmondsworth: Penguin.

Jervis, R. (1978) 'Cooperation under the security dilemma', *World Politics* 30, 2, 167–214.

Jeszensky, G. (1992) 'Nothing quiet on the Eastern Front', *NATO Review*, 40, 3, 7–13.

Joffe, J. (1984) 'Europe's American pacifier', *Foreign Affairs*, 54, 1, 64–82.

Jordan, C. (1991) 'Greenway 1989–90, the foundation of the east European Green Parties', in S. Parkin (ed.) *Green Light on Europe*, London: Heretic Books.

Kaldor, M. (1989) 'The new peace movement and European security', in O. Waever, P. Lemaitre and E. Tromer (eds) *European Polyphony: Perspectives Beyond East–West Confrontation*, London: Macmillan.

Kaplan, F. (1983) *The Wizards of Armageddon*, New York: Simon and Schuster.

Kearns, I. (1991) 'Policies towards Northern Ireland', in S. Croft (ed.) *British Security Policy: The Thatcher Years and the End of the Cold War*, London: Harper Collins.

Kennedy, P. (1988) *The Rise and Fall of the Great Powers: Economic Change and Military Conflict From 1500 to 2000*, London: Fontana Press.

Kenwood, A. and Lougheed, A. (1983) *The Growth of the International Economy, 1820–1980*, London: George Allen and Unwin.

Keohane, R. and Hoffmann, S. (eds) (1991) *The New European Community: Decisionmaking and Institutional Change*, Boulder: Westview Press.

Kissinger, H. (1957) *A World Restored*, London: Gollancz.

Kramer, J. (1983) 'Environmental problems in eastern Europe: the price for progress', *Slavic Review*, 24, 2, 204–20.

Kramer, J. (1991) 'Eastern Europe and the "energy shock" of 1990–91', *Problems of Communism*, May-June, 85–97.

Larrabee, F. (1992) 'Down and out in Warsaw and Budapest: eastern Europe and east–west migration', *International Security*, 16, 4, 5–34.

Larrabee, F. (1992) 'Instability and change in the Balkans', *Survival*, 34, 2, 31–49.

Lijphart, A. (1969) 'Consociational democracy', *World Politics*, 21, 207–25.

Linklater, A. (1990) *Men and Citizens in the Theory of International Relations*, 2nd edn, London: Macmillan.

Linter, V. and Mazey, S. (1991) *The European Community: Economic and Political Aspects*, London: McGraw-Hill.

Locke, J. (1986) *The Two Treatises of Government*, London: Dent, first published 1690.

Lodge, J. (ed.) (1989) *The European Community and the Challenge of the Future*, London: Pinter.

Lowenthal, M. (1991) *Europe: Thinking About a Changed Continent*, Washington, DC: Congressional Research Service Report.

Lukes, S. (1973) *Individualism*, Oxford: Blackwell.

Magris, C. (1990) *Danube. A Sentimental Journey from the Source to the Black Sea*, London: Collins Harvill.

Marsh, D. (1989) *The New Germany*, London: Century Press.

Mathews, J. (1989) 'Redefining Security', *Foreign Affairs*, 68, 2, 162–77.

Matthews, R., Rubinoff, A. and Stein, J. (eds) (1989) *International Conflict and Conflict Management*, 2nd edn, London: Prentice-Hall.

Mayall, J. (1990) *Nationalism and International Society*, Cambridge: Cambridge University Press.

Mayall, J. (1991) 'Non-intervention, self-determination and the "new world order"', *International Affairs*, 67, 3, 421–9.

Mayall, J. (1992) 'Nationalism and international security after the Cold War', *Survival*, 34, 1, Spring, 19–35.

Mayne, R. (1972) *Europe Tomorrow: 16 Europeans Look Ahead*, London: Fontana/Collins.

McCormick, J. (1989) *The Global Environmental Movement: Paradise Regained*, London: Belhaven Press.

McCormick, J. (1991) *British Politics and the Environment*, London: Earthscan.

McInnes, C. (1991) 'The future of arms control in Europe', *Arms Control*, 12, 1, 1–19.

Mearsheimer, J. (1983) *Conventional Deterrence*, Ithaca, New York: Cornell University Press.

Mearsheimer, J. (1990) 'Back to the future: instability in Europe after the Cold War', *International Security*, 41, 1, 5–57.

Mennes, L. and Kol, J. (1988) *European Trade Policies and the Developing World*, London: Croom Helm.

Meyer, S. (1989) 'The sources and prospects of Gorbachev's new political thinking on security', in S. Lynn-Jones, S. Miller and S. Van Evera (eds) *Soviet Military Policy*, Cambridge: MIT Press.

Michnik, A. (1990) 'The moral and spiritual origins of solidarity', in *Without Force or Lies*, San Francisco: Mercury.

Moore, L. (1985) *The Growth and Structure of International Trade Since the Second World War*, Brighton: Harvester Wheatsheaf.

Morgenthau, H. (1972) *Politics Among Nations*, New York: Knopf Press.

Morris, J. (1991) *The Concept of Humanitarian Intervention in International Relations*, MA Dissertation, University of Hull.

Murray, R. (1981) *Multinationals Beyond the Market*, Brighton, Harvester Wheatsheaf.

Neumann, I. and Welsh, J. (1991) The other in European self-definition', *Review of International Studies*, 17, 4, 327–48.

Noort, P. Van Den (1988) 'European integration and agricultural protection', in P. Coffey (ed.) *Main Economic Areas of the EEC – Towards 1992*, Dordercht: Kluwer Academic Publishers.

Northedge, F. (1976) *The International Political System*, London: Faber and Faber.

Nugent, N. (1991) *The Government and Politics of the European Community*, 2nd edn, Basingstoke: Macmillan.

Oakeshott, M. (1939) *The Social and Political Doctrines of Contemporary Europe*, Cambridge: Cambridge University Press.

Olson, M. (1965) *The Logic of Collective Action*, Cambridge: Harvard University Press.

Payne, R. (1991) *The West European Allies, The Third World and US Foreign Policy*, New York: Praeger.

Pearce, D. (1992) 'Economics and the global environmental challenge', in I. Rowlands and M. Greene (eds) *Global Environmental Change and International Relations*, Basingstoke: Macmillan, in association with Millennium, *Journal of International Studies*.

Pierre, A. (1986) *A Widening Atlantic: Domestic Change and Foreign Policy*, New York: Council on Foreign Relations.

Pinder, J. (1991) *The European Community: The Building of a Union*, Oxford: Oxford University Press.

Piscatori, J. (1990) 'The Rushdie affair and the politics of ambiguity', *International Affairs*, 66, 4, 767–89.

Plant, G. (1992) 'Institutional and legal responses to global environmental change', in I. Rowlands and M. Greene (eds) *Global Environmental Change and International Relations*, Basingstoke: Macmillan in association with Millennium, *Journal of International Studies*.

Pollard, S. (1981) *The Integration of the European Economy Since 1815*, London: George Allen and Unwin.

Pond, E. (1992) 'Germany in the new Europe', *Foreign Affairs*, 71, 2.

Ponting, C. (1985) *The Right to Know: The Inside Story of the Belgrano Affair*, London: Sphere.

Porritt, J. and Winner, D. (1988) *The Coming of the Greens*, London: Fontana.

Postel, S. and Flavin, C. (1991) 'Reshaping the global economy', in *State of the World 1991: A Worldwatch Institute Report on Progress Towards a Sustainable Society*, London: Norton.

Powell, Gen. C. (1991) 'Military realities and future security prospects', *RUSI Journal*, 136, 1, 17–21.

Rees, A. (1986) 'The Soviet Union', in R. Vincent (ed.) *Foreign Policy and Human Rights*, Cambridge: Cambridge University Press.

Rees, W. (1991) 'The Anglo-American security relationship', in S. Croft (ed.) *British Security Policy: The Thatcher Years and the End of the Cold War*, London: Harper Collins.

Rich, B. (1990) 'The Emperor's new clothes: the World Bank and environmental reform', *World Policy Journal*, 7, 2.

Robertson, G. (1990) 'Britain in the new Europe', *International Affairs*, 66, 4, 697–703.

Rowlands, I. (1992) 'The international politics of global environmental change', in I. Rowlands and M. Greene (eds) *Global Environmental Change and International Relations*, Basingstoke: Macmillan, in association with Millennium, *Journal of International Studies*.

Rushdie, S. (1988) *The Satanic Verses*, London: Viking.

RUSI (1991) 'Western European Union: who, where, why?', *RUSI Newsbrief*, 11, 4, 27–8.

RUSI (1991a) 'The Ukraine's nascent defence policy', *RUSI Newsbrief*, 11, 12, 89–91.

Salmon, T. (1992) 'Testing times for European political co-operation: the Gulf and Yugoslavia, 1990–1992', *International Affairs*, 68, 2, 233–53.

Schmidt, V. (1990) 'Engineering a critical realignment of the electorate: the case of the Socialists in France', *West European Politics*, 13, 2, 192–216.

Schonfield, A. (1972) *Europe: Journey to an Unknown Destination*, Harmondsworth: Penguin Books.

Shackleton, M. (1990) *Financing the European Community*, London: Pinter Publishers/RIIA.

Sharp, J. (1987) 'After Reykjavik: arms control and the allies', *International Affairs*, 63, 22, 239–59.

Simai, M. (1992) 'Hungarian problems', *Government and Opposition*, 27, 1, 52–66.

Sked, A. (1990) '*A Proposal for European Union*', Occasional Paper No. 9, Bruges Group.

Smith, G. (1990) *Politics in Western Europe*, 5th edn, Aldershot: Dartmouth.

Smolar, A. (1992) 'Democratisation in central-eastern Europe and international security', in New Dimensions of International Security Part 2, *Adelphi Papers*, no. 266, 25–34.

Snyder, J. (1990) 'Averting anarchy in the new Europe', *International Security*, 14, 4, 5–41.

Snyder, J. (1992) 'Nationalism and instability in the former Soviet Union', in S. Croft and P. Williams (eds) *European Security Without the Soviet Union*, London: Frank Cass and Co.

Stavins, R. (1989) 'Harnessing market forces to protect the environment', *Environment*, 31, January.

Taylor, P. (1991) 'The European Community and the state', *Review of International Studies*, 17, 2, 109–25.

Thomas, H. (1973) *Europe; the Radical Challenge*, London: Weidenfeld and Nicolson.

Thomsen, S. and Nicolaides, P. (1991) *The Evolution of Japanese Direct Investment in Europe: Death of a Transistor Salesman*, Brighton: Harvester Wheatsheaf.

Tiersky, R. (1992) 'France in the new Europe', *Foreign Affairs*, 71, 2, 131–47.

Tinbergen, J. and Fischer, D. (1987) *Warfare and Welfare: Integrating Security Policy with Socio-Economic Policy*, London: St Martin.

Tivey, L. (ed.) (1981) *The Nation-State*, Oxford: Martin Robertson.

Ullman, R. (1991) *Securing Europe*, London: Adamantine Press.

Urwin, D. (1991) *The Community of Europe*, Harlow: Longman.

Vaahtoranta, T. (1990) 'Atmospheric pollution as a global policy problem', *Journal of Peace Research*, 27, 2, 169–76.

Vavrousek, J. et al. (1991) 'Ecological policy in Czechoslovakia', in S. Parkin. (ed.) *Green Light on Europe*, London: Heretic Books.

Vayrynan, R. (ed.) (1985) *Policies for Common Security*, London: SIPRI / Taylor and Francis.

Vincent, R. (1986) *Human Rights and International Relations*, RIIA: Cambridge University Press.

Vincent, R. and Wilson, P. (1992) 'Beyond non-intervention' in I. Forbes and M. Hoffmann (eds) *Ethics and Intervention*, London: Macmillan.

Vincent, R. (1991) 'Grotius, human rights and intervention' in A. Roberts, B. Kingsbury and H. Bull (eds) *Hugo Grotius and International Relations*, Oxford: Clarendon Press.

Wams, T. (1991) 'The deceptive appearance of the Dutch environment plan', in S. Parkin (ed.) *Green Light on Europe*, London: Heretic Books.

Weber, C. (1992) 'Reconsidering statehood', *Review of International Studies*, 18, 3, 199–216.

Weller, Marc (1992) 'The international response to the dissolution of the Socialist Federal Republic of Yugoslavia', *American Journal of International Law*, 86, 3, 569–607.

Weston, A., Cable, V. and Hewitt, A. (1980) *The EEC's Generalised System of Preferences*, London: Overseas Development Institute.

Widgren, J. (1990) 'International migration and regional stability', *International Affairs*, 66, 4, 749–66.

Wight, M. (1979) *Power Politics*, Middlesex: Pelican.

Williams, P. and Barker, M. (1988) *Superpower Détente: A Reappraisal*, London, Sage for the Royal Institute of International Affairs.

Wistrich, E. (1991) *After 1992: The United States of Europe*, London: Routledge.

Wohlstetter, A. (1959) 'The delicate balance of terror', *Foreign Affairs* 37, 2, 211–34.

Yannopoulos, G. (ed.) (1986) *Greece and the EEC*, London: Macmillan.

Yannopoulos, G. (ed.) (1989) *European Integration and the Iberian Economies*, London: Macmillan.

Zametica, John (1992) 'The Yugoslav conflict', *Adelphi Papers* no. 270, IISS.

ZumBrunnen, C. (1992) 'The environmental challenges in eastern Europe', in I. Rowlands and M. Greene (eds) *Global Environmental Change and International Relations*, Basingstoke: Macmillan, in association with Millennium, *Journal of International Studies*.

NEWSPAPERS AND WEEKLIES

Atkins, R. (1990) 'Winning the hearts but not enough minds', *Financial Times*, 30 January.

Brummer, A. (1992) 'Lamont pledges foreign aid to assist third world clean up', *The Guardian*, 29 April.

Cowe, R. (1992) 'Banks dip their toes into the green pond', *The Guardian*, 25 April.

Cowe, R. (1992a) 'Business wakes up to the environment', *The Guardian*, 8 May.

The Economist (1984) 'Making a killing', 20 November, pp. 78–9.

The Economist (1988) 'A survey of the internal market', 9 July, p. 58.

The Economist (1989a) 'A survey of Europe's internal market', 8 July, pp. 33–43.

The Economist (1989b) 'Greening Europe: the freedom to be cleaner than the rest', 14 October, pp. 27–34.

The Economist (1990) 'An expanding universe: a survey', 7 July, 1–40.

The Economist (1991a) 'A survey of business in Europe', 8 June, pp. 1–34.

The Economist (1991b) 'The ambush awaiting Japan', 6 July, pp. 71–2.

The Economist (1991c) 'European regional clubs – hello, neighbours', 13 July, p. 55.

The Economist (1991d) 'An inch deeper into the Balkan quagmire', 18 July, p. 39.

The Economist (1991e) 'Workers of the EEC (except Britain) unite', 19 October, p. 80.

The Economist (1991f) 'Lest a fortress arise', 26 October, pp. 105–6; 'European Economic Area; a short shelf life', p.66.

The Economist (1991g) 'The final stretch', 9 November, pp. 120–2.

The Economist (1991h) 'L'etat c'est Europe, a survey of France', 23 November, pp.10–12.

The Economist (1992) 'The morning after the blow fell', 6 June, pp. 41–2.

The Economist (1992a) 'Survey on Spain: discovering the USA', 25 April, p.23.

The Economist (1992b) 'Switzerland joins the queue', 25 May, p.54.

The Economist (1992c) 'Survey on Germany: there she blows', 23 May, p.9.

The Economist (1992d) 'Why the Danes wouldn't', 6 June, p.42.

The Economist (1992e) 'The morning after the blow fell', 6 June, pp.41–2.

The Economist (1992f) 'Pain in France', 11 July, p.15.

The Economist (1992g) 'An inch deeper into the Balkan quagmire', 18 July, p.39.

Gardner, D. (1992) 'EC proposes tax on energy to fight global warming', *Financial Times*, 14 May.

Genscher, H-D. (1992) 'A spirit of solidarity', *Financial Times*, 16 May.

The Guardian (1984) 'Firm abandons workers and strips faculty', 17 April, p.3.

The Guardian (1991a) 'Soaring mark puts ERM under pressure', 19 November, p.15.

The Guardian (1991b) 'US hopes for a Europe "whole and free" but not too independent', 7 December, p.8.

The Guardian (1992) 'Energy plan a "carbon con" ' 16 May.

Heisbourg, F. (1991) 'Europe needs new rules and the teeth to enforce them', *International Herald Tribune*, 10 September.

Hoffmann, S. (1991) 'A state's internal conditions are outsiders' business', *International Herald Tribune*, 27 February.

The Independent (1991) 'CSCE wins right to discuss Soviet crisis', 21 June.

The Independent (1992) 'Pentagon lists – the seven wars', 18 February.

Jane's Defence Weekly (1992) 'ASW gives way to missile defence as US priority', 14 March, p. 437.

Jane's Defence Weekly (1992a) 'US Air Force's new multi-role wings take shape', 28 March, p. 517.

Lascelles, D. (1992) 'Carbon tax faces Europe with steep cost rises', *Financial Times*, 14 May.

Lascelles, D. (1992a) 'World energy producers on trial', *Financial Times*, 14 May.

Montagon, P. (1989) 'Sharp rise on green interest rate: World Bank's efforts to address environmental concerns', *Financial Times*, 26 July.

Mortimer, E. (1992) 'Alternatives to violence', *The Financial Times*, 24 June.

Palmer, J. (1992) 'EC wavers over plan to tax carbon dioxide emissions', *The Guardian*, 30 April.

Palmer, J. (1992a) 'Major to hear Delors plan for handing back powers', *The Guardian*, 23 June.

Reuter (1992) 'Baltic marine ecology pact', *The Guardian*, 10 April.

Schwarz, W. (1990) 'The price of affluence is effluents', *The Guardian*, 3 January.

Schwarz, W. (1988) 'Green issues rise in the East', *The Guardian*, 26 November.

Stephen, C. (1992) 'Sofia's choice: lethal plant or power cuts', *The Guardian*, 14 May.

Theorin, Maj. B. (1992) 'The military', *The Guardian*, 8 May.

Thomas, D. (1990) 'Industry warns on pollution control plans', *Financial Times*, 2 July.

Thompson, J. (1991) 'East Europe's dark dawn', *National Geographic*, 179, 6.

Vidal, J. (1989) 'A bandwagon they all want to jump on', *The Guardian*, 29 December.

Vidal, J. (1992) 'The green dragon', *The Guardian*, 24 April.

Vidal, J. (1992a) 'Eco soundings', *The Guardian*, 1 May.

Vidal, J. (1992b) 'A world shackled by economic chains', *The Guardian*, 8 May.

Vidal, J. (1992c) 'Forty chapter agenda that divides North and South', *The Guardian*, 9 June.

Vidal, J. (1992d) 'Environment monitor for global funding bodies', *The Guardian*, 9 June.

Vidal, J. and Chaterjee, P. (1992) 'All the difference in the world', *The Guardian*, 10 April.

Wolf, J. (1990) 'Poland "used as dumping ground" for toxic waste', *The Guardian*, 12 October.

Zametica, J. (1992) 'War along federal lines', *The Guardian*, 16 April.

CONFERENCE PAPERS

Greene, O. (1992) 'Conflict prevention in the new Europe: Lessons from Yugoslavia', paper presented to the ECPR Conference, University of Limerick, April, p. 3.

Jackson, R. (1992) 'Is there an international community: intervention or isolation?', paper prepared for the Dartmouth College/United Nations Conference on 'National Sovereignty and Collective Intervention', May.

Kramer, J. (1991a) 'Energy and the environment in Eastern Europe', paper presented at the British International Studies Association Conference, Warwick University, December.

Prager, H. (1992) 'The ecosystem and advanced industrial society: is a change occurring in the American strategy towards UNCED?', paper presented at the Annual Meeting of the International Studies Association, Atlanta, Georgia, April.

Wheeler, N. and Morris, J. (1992) 'The UN's policing role in the New World Order', paper presented at the 'New World Order Conference', Richmond College, November. (To be published by the Friedrich Ebert Foundation, forthcoming).

DOCUMENTS AND COMMUNIQUÉS

Document of the Moscow meeting of the Conference on the Human Dimension of the Conference on Security and Co-operation in Europe, (1991) 10 September–4 October.

HMSO (1987) Statement on the Defence Estimates, Vol. I, *Cm 101*, London.

North Atlantic Treaty Organisation (NATO) (1981) *Basic Documents Brussels*, NATO Information Service.

North Atlantic Treaty Organisation (NATO) (1991) *The Alliance's New Strategic Concept*, Press Communiqué S–1(91)85, 7 November.

North Atlantic Treaty Organisation (NATO) (1991a) *Rome Declaration on Peace and Cooperation*, Press Communiqué S–1(91)86, 8 November.

Office for Offical Publications for the European Communities (1990) *Panorama of European Industry*, Luxembourg: Office for Official Publications for the European Communities.

Organisation for Economic Co-operation and Development (OECD) (1989) *Agricultural and Environmental Policies: Opportunities for Integration*, Paris: OECD.

Prague Document on Further Development of CSCE Institutions and Structures (1992) CSCE Prague Council Meeting, 30 January.

Rome Declaration on Peace and Cooperation (1991) Issued by the Heads of State and Government participating in the meeting of the North Atlantic Council, Rome, 7–8 November

US Information Service, London, 13 December 1989, speech by James Baker, Secretary of State, in Berlin.

Index